Praise for *Greater Than You Think*

Pastor Jeff Jenkins doesn't just preach truth, he lives it in the trenches of real life and I'm so blessed to see his humble leadership at our home church. *Greater Than You Think* captures the same hope-filled message that transforms lives every weekend at Anchor Church. As someone without limbs who faces impossible circumstances daily, I know the difference between religious theory and faith that actually works. Jeff offers what I call 'meat-shakes': rich biblical truth that's easy to digest and immediately practical! Whether you're a skeptic, seeker, or seasoned believer, this book will expand your view of God in ways that change everything, because our God truly has NO limits!

—Nick Vujicic
Evangelist & Author, Founder of NickV Ministries

"You can't know God's will until you know God."
I've had the distinct honor of working closely with Pastor Jeff Jenkins for more than ten years as a layman in the church, and I've never known a man more consumed with knowing God and doing His will. It seems obvious that we can't serve the Lord without knowing Him deeply, yet that truth is often forgotten as we try to live out our professed faith. This book will help readers navigate their own doubts and questions about the character of God. Knowing Him better can only lead to a deeper sense of awe, love, trust, and commitment. Read this book.

—Andrew Gwynn
Elder, Anchor Church

Pastor Jeff isn't just my friend and Pastor; he's one of the most gifted communicators I know. Some pastors make theological truths feel like climbing a mountain, but Jeff has a way of bringing those same truths right down to where you live. He takes what's deep and makes it real, relatable, practical, and anchored in everyday life.

Greater Than You Think is exactly that kind of book. It's for anyone who's spiritually hungry but mentally exhausted, for those wrestling with questions about faith, doubt, and who Jesus really is. Jeff writes from a place of lived experience, not theory, making complex truths simple, and spiritual concepts personal.

If you've ever felt weary in your faith or just needed a reason to keep believing, this book will meet you where you are and remind you that Jesus is far greater, more present, and more personal than you think.

—**Brad Crews**
Elder & Executive Lead Pastor, Anchor Church

If the portrait of your Christian walk often looks or feels like a forgery, this book is for you. If the unanswered questions that you are afraid to utter, out of fear of being exposed for your doubts, this book is for you. Jeff's hard-fought experiences reveal how to know that God is real, that He is greater and more able than you can think or imagine, and that He is for YOU.

—**Richard Giannoni**
Elder, Anchor Church

Whether it's been a message, a story, a revelation, or teaching on scripture, there have been so many times that Pastor Jeff Jenkins has said something that I wish I had written down… What a gift to the world to have a book containing some of Jeff's wisdom and insight! In this hour, more than ever, the body of Christ needs strong leaders who walk in humility, and the fear of The Lord, to help shepherd His bride back to the truth of who God is. Pastor Jeff is one of those leaders. I am honored to be pastored by Jeff, not because of the obvious gift of teaching he carries on the platform… but because of the fruit I see first in his marriage, his family, and in his personal passion to follow Jesus no matter the season, and at any cost. *Greater Than You Think* is no doubt an overflow from decades of time in secret place at the feet of Jesus… and I pray it leads many to see the beautiful heart of The Father in a deeper and truer way.

—Cammie Avers
Anchor Worship Pastor (Songwriter of "Give Me Jesus")

It's one thing to study, search, and gather information for a book — but it's another thing entirely to seek the Lord for language that expresses what He's doing in your heart. Over the years, I've watched Jeff Jenkins intentionally humble himself before the Lord, submitting again and again to the refining process required to be entrusted with true treasure from Heaven. God is revealing Himself to Jeff, and these pages carry both the truth and the treasure born out of that sacred intimacy.

—Zac Rowe
Anchor Executive Lead Pastor of Worship
(Songwriter of "Who Else")

GREATER

THAN

YOU

THINK

Embracing a God
Bigger Than Your Box

JEFF JENKINS

ANCHOR

COLLECTIVE

ISBN: 979-8-9932552-0-0 paperback
ISBN: 979-8-9932552-1-7 hardcover
ISBN: 979-8-9932552-2-4 eBook

While the author makes every effort to provide accurate URLs at the time of printing for external or third-party Internet websites, neither they nor the publisher assume any responsibility for changes or errors made after publication.

myanchorchurch.com
@myanchorchurch

Cover design and typeset by Peyton Sepeda, WildCreativePublishing.com

Printed in the United States of America
26 27 28—5 4 3 2

TABLE OF CONTENTS

TRIBUTE

TO CHARLIE'S WIFE, his children, his Turning Point team, and to every person whose life has been marked by his ministry:

I write these words with a heart full of honor and gratitude. Your husband, your father, your leader, your friend lived as a gift not just to you, but to millions of us who watched with awe and admiration as he stood boldly for truth in a world that often rewards compromise. I know that the cost of that courage was not his alone. You clearly bore it with him. Every sacrifice, every late night, every pressure and headline, every moment of unseen weight was carried by you too. For that, we honor you.

We honor you, Erika. Your strength, lioness heart, resolve and devotion is inspirational to us all. We can see how your love and partnership fueled Charlie's courage to be strong. He was anchored in love at home. We honor his children, who now carry the legacy of a father whose voice will echo through generations. We honor his Turning Point family, who stood shoulder to shoulder with him, often under fire, but never without faith. And we honor the countless students and young adults who sat under his words, who found courage to believe, to think, and to live differently because Charlie Kirk called them higher.

As I dedicate this book, I want you to know that I do so with you in mind. Because his ministry was so much greater than the debates, stages, or headlines. His legacy was about Jesus and love for all people. Charlie has ignited millions of young bold warriors reclaim truth, rediscover faith, and rebuild their lives on foundations that cannot be shaken.

Here is what I valued most about Charlie and why I believe those values matter so deeply in this moment, and why this book is written for such a time as this.

Boldness in Truth. Charlie never flinched when it came to truth. He believed God's sovereignty was bigger than cultural backlash. God is always in control, though He doesn't always take control and Charlie lived like he believed it. That boldness inspired others to live courageously, to open their mouths when silence would have been easier. This book carries the same heartbeat: truth that refuses to bend, anchored in the sovereignty of God.

Faith with Conviction. Charlie's faith wasn't a private thing, it was everything to him. It was deep and obvious. He lived and led with conviction that God cannot fail, and that His Word is trustworthy even when the world is hostile. For me, that same conviction carried me through doubt, through tests of fire and eventually surrender. It is the reason I write: to show that when your thoughts betray you, God remains faithful.

Love for Freedom. Charlie stood for freedom because he knew freedom comes from God. Not just national liberty, but the freedom of the soul. God cannot lack. He gives us everything we need for life and godliness, and that abundance means we don't have to live in bondage to fear or sin. Charlie's passion for freedom mirrors the message of this book: a life that transcends cultural captivity because it is rooted in the Spirit of God.

Honor and Respect for Legacy. In an age that mocks what is sacred, Charlie restored honor to God, to family, to faith, to country. He reminded us that God's ways are eternal, steadfast, unchanging. God cannot change, and His constancy is our anchor in chaos. In this book, I seek to help readers discover that honoring the ancient paths of God is not weakness, it is strength.

Courageous Leadership for the Next Generation. Charlie's greatest gift was calling forth leaders. He believed young people are the leaders God has designed to impact the present. God cannot be defeated, and His Spirit empowers us to live as more than conquerors. Charlie called a generation to stand, and my prayer is that this book will do the same: to awaken a new wave of bold, Spirit-filled leaders who rise above fear and live greater than they think.

To his wife, his children, his team, and his friends … know this: His life was a seed, and seeds don't die when they fall into the ground. They bloom. They multiply. His values of boldness, conviction, freedom, honor, and courage reflect the very attributes of God Himself, which are eternal and unshakable.

This book, *Greater Than You Think*, is dedicated in part to you, because it carries forward the same mission: to help a generation live beyond shallow thinking, beyond fragile feelings, beyond cultural confusion. It's a call into the fullness of faith, truth, and Spirit-led life. Charlie showed us that when you anchor yourself in the eternal character of God, you stand on foundations that cannot be shaken. My prayer is that these pages will honor his life by awakening yours.

INTRODUCTION
What You Think Is Only Part of You

IN THE WINTER of 2002, I was on my way home from Nashville, TN, to Greenville, KY. It was about 10:00 p.m. when I pulled over on the side of the road. Every overpass I drove under had become a moment of despair and turmoil. Every few minutes I was having sincere onslaughts of unbelief mixed with increasing thoughts of not wanting to live anymore. I thought I was done with faith. At twenty-eight years old, having been a senior pastor for only one year, I was in way over my head and under serious attack.

I was working on my master's degree in theology and had just finished the fourth three-hour intensive course on Biblical Criticism. My professor excelled at stirring up questions about the reliability of the Bible. Unfortunately, he was inadequate at answering my sincere questions—doing more harm than good, at least with me. I needed serious help or I wasn't going to make it.

My plan was to leave the faith completely and go to law school. My darker thoughts weren't even interested in living anymore. I shared what I was going through with my wife, Sarah. She couldn't empathize with my struggle. When I told her, "I don't think Peter wrote Second Peter and I don't think...," her response wasn't cold-hearted, but it was cooler than I wanted. She definitively said, "Well, you better figure it out if you want to be a preacher." That's hilarious now, but it wasn't then.

A few months later, I was at the Parish Hermitage in St. Amant, Louisiana, with my therapist, Dr. Eddie Parish. He had been my therapist since 1995. We sat at a large table in his open kitchen and dining area, facing a giant glass wall with Spanish moss-filled oak trees surrounding the house. I was drinking a root beer. He was drinking a beer.

I began to unload my burden of doubt, unbelief, and crippling anxiety. I worried about saying things that would hurt his faith, but my concerns didn't hold me back. I unloaded for about forty-five minutes straight, going from Genesis to Revelation. I poured out everything I could think of that served as evidence in my mind that God isn't real. I was in a genuine faith crisis and desperately needed help.

I started with Moses's divine revelation of Creation and the 1,500-year history of Israel before his own birth. I critiqued the law codes and compared Israel's laws with the influence of Mesopotamian moral codes and stories. I questioned the credibility of the major and minor prophets, accusing them of being edited to fit history. I even criticized Jesus for knowing Scripture and intentionally fulfilling prophecy to claim deity. I challenged the Resurrection, suggesting the seal and guard were placed at an already-empty tomb. I had somewhat concluded that Joseph of Arimathea never buried the body or somehow retrieved it, creating a legendary tale that the disciples naively believed. I noted that Joseph conveniently went silent afterward. I theorized that the disciples' encounters were more like the denial and bargaining stages of grief, accompanied by emotional hallucinations—supported by the fact that even some who witnessed the ascension still doubted. I thought the disciples themselves were genuine and their convictions deepened through persecution. I accused the Catholic Church of using religious and papal power to combine church and state, arguing that their process for forming the canon of Scripture wasn't reliable because it was founded on a hunger for power.

I was unwavering and incapable of doubting my own doubts, powerless against my internal arrogance. I didn't even know how to express what I was thinking from a place of curiosity anymore. I didn't want more information—I just wanted to vent.

Then there was about a minute of absolute silence. I broke it by asking, "Well, what do you think?"

Dr. Parish, with a Gandalf-like long goatee, and a long grey ponytail tightly pulled back, uncrossed his legs, leaned forward toward me, paused another few seconds while staring right into the bullseye of my soul and said, "Hell, I don't know. Want another root beer?"

I burst into a relieved laughter. As he got me another root beer, I thought, *This is the first time in my life I've ever felt the power of someone else being okay with knowing what's really in my brain.*

A few months later, I shared an edited version of my struggle with another leader.

He asked, "So, Jeff—do you believe in God?"

"No, I don't think I do," I replied.

"What if you do?"

"I don't think I do."

"What if you do?"

Now curious, I asked, "What do you mean, 'What if you do'? I don't think I do."

He then asked, "Does part of you believe?"

I quickly nodded, "Yeah."

Then he asked a question that changed my life:

> Jeff, what if that part of you is the most real part of you? You are spirit, Jeff. You have a soul and you live in a body. The doubts you're expressing are all in the cognitive part of who you are, and that's only a small part of your mind. But you're so much more than just "I think." God is spirit, and you're designed to know Him in your spirit. Your spirit is designed to lead your soul, and your soul leads your body. You're closer to knowing Him than you think.

The most real part of me is my spirit. It's already saved. It's already seated in the heavenlies with Christ. It is already made perfect. It is already whole. It already knows God. The rest of me is still catching up, and I'm now enjoying the journey of faith with freedom from the crippling power of doubt and unbelief.

This journey was the beginning of me learning to let God out of the box of my very limited thinking—the journey that has led to me knowing Him as the God who is *Greater Than You Think.*

My deepest life message is centered in knowing Him personally and being known by Him—to the degree that hope comes alive in people who have lost it.

Friedrich Nietzsche, the German philosopher, famously said, "Hope is the worst of all evils, for it only prolongs the torments of man."[1] He's partially right. Even Proverbs 13:12 says, "Hope deferred makes the heart sick, but a dream fulfilled is a tree of life" (NLT). Hope is a terrible thing when it's disconnected from what outlasts you. Hope must be rooted in the dream that outlasts you. That dream is knowing Jesus, the True and Living Anchor for our soul. He is the Hope that outlasts us. He is the Dream of Life. And that Dream isn't just ideal— *it's real.*

> ## My deepest life message is centered in knowing Him personally and being known by Him.

There's an experiential reality in knowing Jesus as our Living Hope. His dream comes alive in us. The dream is tangible. He is knowable.

---

1   Friedrich Nietzsche, *Human, All Too Human: A Book for Free Spirits,* trans. R. J. Hollingdale (Cambridge: Cambridge University Press, 1996), section I.71. Originally published in German in 1878 as *Menschliches, Allzumenschliches: Ein Buch für freie Geister.*

We can experience Him as Hope that is alive and well. The closer we move toward our Hope, the more we know it's alive and well.

This book touches the core of who I am. It isn't just a book—it's the beginning of unpacking my life message. My personal desire is for every young adult seeker or believer to know the hope to which they are called. I want every pastor who has tapped the brakes on faith to know He's bigger than you think. I want every parent struggling to relate to their loved ones with hope to know the best is ahead. I want every entrepreneur clashing against one level of resistance after another to believe there's nothing greater than persevering forward as if Heaven matters and the promises of God are true.

If you're ready for this journey, then repeat this simple prayer:

Lord, have mercy. I want to know you.

This prayer is deeper than it is long. But if you mean it, then your life is about to change—and so is the level of your influence.

Discovering the God Who Is

On Saturday, September 5, 1992, I ran onto the field in Death Valley—Louisiana State University's Tiger Stadium—for the first time. We were facing the No. 7 ranked Texas A&M Aggies before a crowd of 69,313 fans, well short of the stadium's 80,150 capacity. In the midst of that electric atmosphere, I tripped and caused a 20-man pile-up under the goal post.

It wasn't the size of the crowd that made me fall—it was the overwhelming energy of the stadium itself. We lost that day, 31–22, but honestly, my spectacular face-plant probably got more attention than half the plays.

The next afternoon during a light conditioning workout inside the empty stadium, something clicked.

"You know what's crazy?" I said to my teammates, while I was still nursing a bruised ego from the previous day's performance. "During games, we're so locked in on the field that nobody really notices this stadium. But the stadium itself is actually more massive, more impressive, and more permanent than anything that happens on the playing field."

Thirty-three years later, I recognize that moment as a profound realization—one that has shaped my understanding of Jesus and ministry ever since. The reality of who Jesus actually is exceeds everything else we get caught up in. He's infinitely greater, more impressive, more enduring, and ultimately more significant than any circumstance in our daily lives.

Sometimes it takes tripping over your own feet in front of 69,000 people to gain some perspective.

That incident at the football game made it clear to me that we spend so much time focused on our personal "game"—concerned with how we appear to others, who's watching us, and who we're competing against. We become fixated on what's happening on our small patch of turf during what is, in truth, just a brief moment in time.

The problem is, many of us have a limited, distorted, or incomplete view of Jesus. Yes, He was fully human and is now resurrected, glorified, and has ascended as man—but He's also fully God. He didn't complete His work in this world only to be diminished into our image—reduced to a source of convenient favor, an affirmer of our preferences, an enabler of our pet sins, or merely a support system for our small dreams.

Jesus was and is God. During His earthly life, He embodied all the Divine attributes as God in flesh, demonstrating them through the Spirit and in relationship with the Father. When we embrace a theology that emphasizes certain aspects of His character while neglecting others, we're left with an unbalanced and incomplete understanding that affects every dimension of our faith.

I've seen this play out countless times in pastoral ministry. People whose view of God as primarily judgmental leaves them paralyzed by shame and fear. Others whose conception of God as only loving leads them into moral compromise and confusion. Some emphasize God's sovereignty to the point of fatalism, and others focus on His grace to the exclusion of His holiness.

These distorted views of God don't just create theological problems; they produce practical consequences. Jesus came to reveal how humans functionally and positionally relate God. So often we shrink Jesus down to fit our needs—turning Him into a personal assistant, a yes-man for our decisions, or just backup for our plans. However, if we get Jesus wrong, we get everything else wrong.

That's why exploring the attributes of God—the essential characteristics that define who He is—matters so much. This isn't just a theological exercise for seminary students or Bible scholars. It's an important journey for anyone who wants to really know God and live according to who He actually is.

What Are Divine Attributes?

Before we dive into specific attributes, let's clarify what we mean by this term. Divine attributes are the perfect qualities or characteristics that belong to God and make Him different from everything and everyone else. They're not just what God does but *who God is at His core.*

Theologians have different ways of organizing God's characteristics. Some separate them into traits God shares with people (like love and wisdom) versus traits that belong only to God (like being everywhere at once). Others group them by God's power versus God's goodness.

These categories can be useful, but I'm taking a simpler approach. We'll look at *seven key characteristics* (attributes) that give us a solid foundation for understanding who God is. These aren't the only traits God has, but they're a good starting point for knowing Him better and responding to Him in the right way.

What Lies Ahead

In this book, we'll explore these seven characteristics of God and see how Jesus showed them in His own life.

Chapter 1: Higher Than Your Agenda— The Holiness of God

We'll start with God's holiness—how He's completely different from everything else. Looking at Jesus's first miracle at the wedding in Cana, we'll see how God's holiness works with God's timing, methods, and purpose. All of these are bigger than our human plans.

Chapter 2: The Rock That Never Moves— The Immutability of God

Next, we'll look at how God never changes—His character, promises, and plans stay the same no matter what happens around us. Through the story of the woman caught in adultery, we'll see how God's consistency can give us stability in an unstable world.

Chapter 3: Supreme Ruler— The Sovereignty of God

Then we'll look at God's sovereignty—how He's in charge of everything. Through Jesus feeding the 5,000 and walking on water, we'll see how God's control works on both a universal scale and in our personal lives.

Chapter 4: When God Doesn't Take Control— Personal Sovereignty

Building on God's sovereignty, we'll explore the puzzle of our freedom—how God can be sovereign while our choices still matter. Looking at Jesus' encounters with different doubters shows us how God engages each of us personally.

Chapter 5: Known By Name— The Omniscience of God

Next, we'll look at God's perfect knowledge—how He knows all things, including everything about us. Using Jesus's encounter with the Samaritan woman at the well, we'll see how being fully known and fully loved transforms us.

Chapter 6: Never Alone— The Omnipresence of God

We'll then look at how God is everywhere at all times, including the different ways we experience His presence. Mary's anointing of Jesus shows us how worship recognizes and invites God's presence.

Chapter 7: Strength Under Control— The Omnipotence of God

We'll study God's unlimited power, especially how it works not through raw force but through perfectly controlled strength. The picture of the Lion and the Lamb in Revelation helps us understand both sides of God's power.

Chapter 8: Living In Response— Practical Application

Last, we'll see how knowing these characteristics transforms everyday life—how we see ourselves, make decisions, pray, and relate to others. We'll cover practical steps for living with a true picture of who God is.

———

In each chapter, I'll tell stories from my life and the lives of people I've served as a pastor. These aren't just abstract concepts to think about—they're living truths that have transformed real people, and they can transform you too.

Why Do You Need to Know All This?

You might be wondering: *Why spend time studying God's attributes? Wouldn't it be better for us to focus on practical Christian living—how to improve our relationships, overcome temptations, or become more effective servants?*

Those practical matters are important. But here's the truth I've found in over twenty-five years of ministry: Nothing is more practical than knowing who God really is. Your view of God will shape everything else in your life.

If you see God first as a demanding taskmaster, then you'll respond out of duty and fear. If you view Him mainly as a cosmic buddy, then you'll treat Him with too casually. If you look at Him as distant and uninvolved, then you'll pray without expecting Him to really do anything. If you see Him as erratic and unpredictable, then you'll live with chronic anxiety.

But when you begin to see God the way He truly is—in the full spectrum of His character—everything changes. You'll worship with more authenticity. You'll grow more confident in your prayers. You'll serve

Him because you're genuinely grateful and not just because you feel obligated. Your relationships will reflect more of His character. Your personal struggles will find their place within God's larger purposes.

> ## Your view of God will shape everything else in your life.

This journey toward knowing God more fully isn't just about gaining information. It's about transformation. As Paul writes in 2 Corinthians 3:18,

> And we all, who with unveiled faces contemplate the Lord's glory, are being transformed into his image with ever-increasing glory, which comes from the Lord, who is the Spirit (NIV).

The more clearly we see who God is, the more fully we become who He has created us to be. That's the promise and purpose of this book—not just to know about God intellectually, but to know Him personally in ways that completely reshape us.

How to Get the Most from This Book

Before we get into the meat of the book, let me offer *five tips* that will help you get the most out of it:

1. Read with an open Bible. I'll be referencing a lot of Scripture passages in each chapter. Take time to look them up, read them in context, and then allow God's Word to speak directly to you.

2. Read with an open heart. This book isn't academic; it's deeply personal. Be willing to take a serious look at how your current understanding of God might be incomplete or distorted. Ask the Holy Spirit to show you the truth and correct your understanding.

3. Read in community. While you can certainly benefit from reading this book alone, you'll get even more out of it when you discuss it with others. Each chapter includes questions for personal reflection and group discussion. Consider reading with friends, family, or a small group so you can interact and get feedback from other voices.

4. Read with patience. Some concepts we'll explore can be really challenging to get a handle on. Don't rush through the hard parts or become frustrated when certain ideas take more time for you to process. This journey of knowing God takes a lifetime, and it can't be microwaved.

5. Read with expectation. God really wants to be known. He isn't hiding from you or playing hard to get. Approach this book with confidence—the same God who created you also wants you to know Him.

A Personal Invitation

As we start this journey together, I'm offering my personal invitation—not just for you to learn about God's attributes but for you to have a genuine encounter with the living God.

This book isn't meant just to inform you; its goal is to transform you. As I write these words, I am praying for you right now. I am asking God to give you understanding, but even more I'm asking Him to reveal Himself to you.

The great reformer Martin Luther said there is a big difference between the "God preached" and the "God experienced." We need both. Good theology matters a lot, but it must move from your head to your heart to your hands—from intellect to experience to action.

So as you read, don't just collect information. Create some space and time to receive revelation. Don't just analyze concepts. Invite an encounter. Don't just examine God's attributes. Worship the One who possesses them all.

Because in the end, I didn't write this book to make you a really smart theologian. I created it so you could meet a Person—the infinite, eternal, all-glorious God who has revealed Himself to us and invites us into relationship with Himself.

So let's discover the God who truly is—beyond our assumptions, above our expectations, and greater than our imaginations. As we do, we'll find that knowing Him changes everything else.

"For from him and through him and to him are all things. To him be glory forever. Amen" (Romans 11:36 ESV).

1
HIGHER THAN YOUR AGENDA

The Holiness of God

THE FIRST TIME I remember encountering God's holiness as a pastor, I definitely wasn't ready for it.

I was serving as Senior Pastor of the Elkton Road Church in Greenville, Kentucky. This was my wife, Sarah's home church. I was in my second year of preaching full-time, and I thought everything was going well. Our little country church was growing, we had our first new-born baby, Shelby, and I was starting to feel more confident in my role as a pastor. I had a big vision, strategy maps in every file on my computer, and more ambition than I knew what to do with.

Then came what I now call my "Isaiah 6 moment."

Late one morning, I was alone in my office praying. I was wrestling with my faith and my calling. I began telling God about frustrations with my faith and all sorts of other struggles I was having. What started as routine prayer and study time shifted suddenly as I started to feel an overwhelming sense of God's presence taking over my attitude and my view of purpose. The only way I can describe it is that everything else—my plans, the sermon coming up, my agenda, my very life itself—all these things felt small in an instant.

Before I knew it, I found myself face down on the carpet, not out of religious duty or habit, but because I couldn't stand or even sit upright in the weight of that moment. For perhaps the first time in my life,

I truly understood what Isaiah meant when he encountered God's holiness and cried out, "Woe is me! For I am lost; for I am a man of unclean lips, and I dwell in the midst of a people of unclean lips; for my eyes have seen the King, the Lord of hosts!" (Isaiah 6:5 ESV).

That was a holy moment. It marked me. Since then, I've had several more close holy encounters. These moments have shaped everything about how I understand repentance, awakening, calling, God, and ministry. I realized I had been working so hard to be a "preacher," when I really needed to be known and sent from God. I kept wrestling with theology as a mental operation, but I was dealing with something much higher than the human mind. My reasoning kept colliding with God's presence.

This is what holiness does—it messes up our careful plans and replaces them with something far better, higher, and more amazing than anything we could have constructed on our own.

What Holiness Really Means

When you hear the word "holy," what come to your mind?

For a lot of people, holiness stirs up images of stern-faced religious folks, wagging fingers of judgment, or perhaps impossibly perfect saints with halos around their heads like you see in old paintings. We've reduced holiness to a churchy self-righteous caricature: don't drink, don't smoke, don't cuss, don't dance—I grew up in the church of Christ. The old joke goes that we weren't supposed to have pre-marital sex because it might lead to dancing. I knew a lot about morality and not much about holiness.

When we think about holiness as mostly good morals and good manners, it's like describing the Grand Canyon as "a big hole in Arizona." We run the great risk of missing everything that matters about God and the Christian life.

The Hebrew word translated 'holiness' is *Kadesh*. This word shows up all over the Old Testament, and it basically means "set apart" or "other." When we apply that word to God, it means He's completely separate from and above everything else in the entire universe. He's in a category all by Himself.

Think about this: *kadesh* is the only word in that Bible that is repeated three times in a row. It's not repeated like that just for emphasis. Instead it's a way Bible writers were turning the volume up all the way. Any word repeated twice in Scripture is strong and loud, but three times is deafening. In Isaiah 6:3, the seraphim don't just say "holy," or even "holy, holy." They cry out "Holy, holy, holy is the LORD of hosts; the whole earth is full of his glory!" (Isaiah 6:3 ESV). Think of that as so loud it would make your ears ring.

In Revelation 4:8, the apostle John takes this same approach in describing heavenly beings who "day and night they never cease to say, 'Holy, holy, holy, is the Lord God Almighty, who was and is and is to come!'" (Revelation 4:8 ESV).

So holiness isn't just one attribute among many—it's *the attribute* that defines all others. That means when God is described as "holy, holy, holy," we're being told that holiness is His most essential characteristic.

If I asked you to name God's most important attribute, what would you say? A lot of people would say "love." Some might say "mercy" or "grace" or "sovereignty." While of those are important words to describe God, the Bible puts holiness right at the center of who God is. All of God's other attributes flow from His holiness.

> Holiness isn't just one attribute among many—it's *the attribute* that defines all others.

Let me clear something up that gets a lot of people confused: *holiness isn't just moral purity,* though it certainly includes that. Even more important, God's holiness means He is absolutely unique. He is completely "other" and transcends everything else He ever created. You can put God versus us on a bar chart with Him high and us low. We can't even be on the same chart. He's not good while we're less good. No, He is one of a kind—He is the Creator, and we are the created.

Jesus: Holiness in Skin and Bones

This is what makes God becoming flesh in the Man Jesus (the Incarnation) so mind-blowing. When Jesus was born as a real human baby, the completely transcendent, most holy God of the universe put on human flesh, walked among us, and moved in next door. That what John 1:14 tells us; it says that "the Word became flesh and dwelt among us" (John 1:14 ESV). He literally "tabernacled" or "pitched His tent" among us.

In Jesus, the holy, holy, holy God of the universe—who is so transcendently other that even the seraphim cover their faces in His presence—put on flesh and moved into the neighborhood! Think about it this way: Jesus came to live on *your* street.

In the Old Testament, God's presence traveled with and dwelled in the Tabernacle. In that tent of worship a thick black curtain separated the Holy of Holies from the people, including the priest. In fact, the high priest was the only one who could step behind that curtain, and he was only allowed to do it once a year. But through Jesus' death on the cross, God's holiness is no longer hidden behind the curtain. Jesus, who was 100% God, walked down the dusty roads of Galilee and sat for dinner with tax collectors and sinners.

Take that in for a minute. The holy, holy, holy God of all creation—who is so transcendently other that even the seraphim cover their faces in His presence—clothed Himself in flesh and got involved in people's lives.

What's so incredible about Jesus is that He is all the holiness the Bible talks about while still being completely approachable and relatable to ordinary people. The religious leaders who were around during Jesus' time on earth made up their own version of holiness. They had a lot of right rules that separated the "good" people from the "sinners." But Jesus stood their moral standards on their head when He showed what holiness really looks like, and it wasn't what anyone expected.

> In Jesus, the holy, holy, holy God of the universe put on flesh and moved into the neighborhood!

For us to understand Jesus' kind of holiness, let's look at a story that might seem like an odd choice at first—the wedding at Cana in John chapter 2.

Water into Wine: Holiness in Action

If you've read the gospels, you know the basics of this story. Jesus attends a wedding with His mother. The wine runs out earlier than expected, which was a major social faux pas in that culture. Mary learns of the problem, so she tells Jesus about it. I'll skip over some of the details, but in the end Jesus turns six large stone jars of water into fine wine, saving the wedding celebration and revealing His glory.

But there's so much more happening in this story that reveals the true nature of holiness. John tells us this was the "first of his signs." Don't miss the significance of that phrase. Of all the ways Jesus could have begun His public ministry—healing the sick, raising the dead, teaching deep truths—He chose to solve a hospitality crisis at a wedding reception. Why? Because true holiness isn't so rigid that it's detached from real life and genuine human problems. It comes into our lives—

even our parties—and changes ordinary experiences into something extraordinary.

Look at where this miracle happens. These water containers were six stone jars normally used for Jewish rites of purification. They weren't just ordinary water jugs. They represented a religious system that required ceremonial cleansing, which was the old traditional way to think about holiness. Inside those jars, Jesus turned ordinary water into extraordinary wine. It's a powerful symbol, which reinforces that Jesus didn't come to abolish the law but to fulfill it. He came to transform religion from empty ritual into joyful relationship.

And think about the quality of the wine Jesus creates. The master of the feast exclaims, "Everyone serves the good wine first, and when people have drunk freely, then the poor wine. But you have kept the good wine until now" (John 2:10 ESV). Jesus doesn't just fix the problem; He does something beyond what's expected or deserved. That's grace, which flows directly from His holiness.

This may seem like a simple story, but we learn *three important truths that will completely change how we understand holiness.*

1. The Timing: Holiness Has a Divine Schedule

In this story, something fascinating happens between Jesus and His mother. When Mary comes to Jesus to tell Him the wine has run out, He answers her with what might sound like a rebuke: "Woman, what does this have to do with me? My hour has not yet come" (John 2:4 ESV).

Does Jesus' response seem harsh? We might think so as modern readers, but He wasn't being disrespectful. "Woman" was a term of great respect in that culture. What Jesus was establishing an important truth about holiness—it operates on God's timetable, not ours.

Mary wanted Jesus to act immediately to solve the problem. Jesus was making it clear that even though He would help out in this crisis, He wasn't going to be controlled or manipulated by human schedules or agendas. His "hour"—the time God the Father chose for Jesus' full revelation and sacrifice—wasn't going to happen just because humans demanded it.

That's a really hard truth for us to accept about God's holiness. Our culture is all about instant gratification. People want solutions *"right now!"* So they will pray, but if God doesn't answer immediately, they give up or come up with their own solutions.

But holiness means God's timing is perfect, even when it doesn't fit with what we want or expect. Throughout the gospels, we see Jesus keeps saying things like, "My time has not yet come" or "The hour has come." He kept His own divine schedule, and it didn't change because of human pressure.

In John 5:19, Jesus makes this even clearer when He says, "The Son can do nothing of his own accord, but only what he sees the Father doing" (John 5:19 ESV). Jesus didn't operate independently, following His own ideas or giving into others' demands. He acted in perfect unity with the Father's will and timing.

Consider how this applies to your own life. How many times have you gotten frustrated or felt anxious because God wasn't working on your schedule? Maybe you're waiting for healing, for a relationship to be restored, for a job opportunity, or for clarity about a decision. You've prayed, you've sought counsel, you've done everything you know to do, but Heaven seems silent.

When Heaven seems silent, it doesn't mean God is absent. It means He's up to something holy. God is operating according to a perfect timetable you can't see yet. His ways are higher than your ways; His thoughts higher than your thoughts (Isaiah 55:8–9). Holiness means trusting God's timing even when it makes no sense to you.

There are typically *three reasons* we get offended by God's timing:

1. We think He's too slow or too fast. Either we're impatient for Him to act, or we aren't ready when He suddenly moves. But God's timing is never off—it's our perception that's limited. He's up to something holy.

2. His timing is disruptive to our plans. God rarely operates according to our carefully plotted life plans. When He intervenes, we often have to adjust our schedules, priorities, and expectations. Holiness disrupts our agenda with a better one. He's up to something holy.

3. His timing remains mysterious. Sometimes we simply can't understand why God chooses to act when He does. Holiness means accepting that God sees the big picture of time while we see only a few pixels. He's up to something holy.

> ## God's timing is never off—
> ## it's our perception that's limited.

In the story of the wedding at Cana, Jesus did eventually solve the problem, but He did it on the Father's terms and according to His timing. This wasn't just a miracle about wine—it was about setting the tone from the very beginning of His ministry. Jesus would only work according to His Father's timetable, not based on human expectations.

This is one reason a lot of people struggle in surrendering fully to God. We want a God who works according to our schedules and preferences. But true holiness is higher than our agenda. When we genuinely encounter God's holiness, we will stop demanding that He fit into our timelines and instead align ourselves with His timing.

2. The Way: Holiness Has a Divine Method

The second truth we can discover from the wedding at Cana is that holiness has its own methodology—its own way of doing things. It doesn't just work according to a different schedule; it operates in an entirely different way than we would with our limited human wisdom.

Look at how Jesus solved the wine problem: He told the servants to fill six stone water jars, each holding twenty to thirty gallons, with water. Then He instructed them to draw some out and take it to the master of the feast. From a human perspective, this makes no logical sense. Water doesn't solve a wine shortage. The servants must have been confused, perhaps even embarrassed, by these instructions.

Imagine being one of those servants. Your job and reputation are on the line. The wedding celebration is in crisis mode. And then this young rabbi tells you to go and fill jars with water and then serve it as if it were wine? That seems like a recipe for disaster, not salvation.

But this is exactly how holiness often works. It asks us to do things that don't seem like they make any sense. It calls us to act in ways that other people might think are foolish or embarrassing.

Remember what God told Joshua for the Israelites to conquer Jericho? God said to march around the city walls for seven days and then shout (Joshua 6:1–5). That's not conventional military strategy, and no one teaches that at Westpoint. Or how about when Jesus told Peter to find tax money in a fish's mouth (Matthew 17:27)? Or when He instructed a blind man to wash mud from his eyes in the pool of Siloam (John 9:7)? These divine instructions look kind of bizarre if we judge them by human standards.

In Matthew's gospel, Jesus lays out the big differences between the way of religion and the way of holiness. In the Sermon on the Mount, several times He says, "You have heard it said ... but I tell you ..." He takes what people thought they understood about righteousness and puts it on a completely different level.

Here's some examples of Him doing just that:

- "You have heard it said, 'You shall not murder'... But I tell you that anyone who is angry with a brother or sister will be subject to judgment" (Matthew 5:21–22 NIV).

- "You have heard it said, 'You shall not commit adultery.' But I tell you that anyone who looks at a woman lustfully has already committed adultery with her in his heart" (Matthew 5:27–28 NIV).

- "You have heard it said, 'Love your neighbor and hate your enemy.' But I tell you, love your enemies and pray for those who persecute you" (Matthew 5:43–44 NIV).

In each case, Jesus is saying, "The way you've been taught to think about this is too low, too limited. My way is higher."

This higher way of holiness tends to bother us for several reasons:

- **We love comfort.** Jesus says, "If anyone would come after me, let him deny himself and take up his cross daily and follow me" (Luke 9:23 ESV). Holiness isn't comfortable—it calls us to sacrificial living, which goes against our natural desire for ease and pleasure.

- **We crave self-preservation.** The way of holiness often requires us to die to ourselves, to put others' needs above our own, to give up what we think we deserve. This goes against our instinct for self-protection.

- **We want control.** Human nature desperately wants to keep up the illusion that we can control our own lives and circumstances. But holiness tells us we have to surrender to God's way of doing things, even when they don't make sense to us.

I remember counseling a couple whose marriage was in serious trouble. Both had valid complaints and grievances against the other. During one particularly tense session, I felt that God wanted me to share what seemed like crazy advice: "For the next thirty days, I want each of you to outdo the other in showing honor and meeting needs—without expectation that your partner will do anything in return."

They looked at me like I'd lost my mind. The husband said, "That's not fair! Why should I serve her when she's the one who ..." And then wife gave a similar response.

But that's exactly how the way of holiness works. It defies human logic. It doesn't start by considering what is fair or what "I deserve." It operates according to grace. Eventually, this couple decided to try following my advice—not because it made sense, but because nothing else had worked up to that point. The relationship was changed dramatically, and it was nothing short of miraculous.

When the servants at Cana decided to obey Jesus's strange instructions, they participated in His miracle. They became conduits through whom God showed His power precisely because they set aside their own understanding and followed the way of Jesus..

Holiness invites us to do the same. It asks, "Will you trust My methods even when they go against your understanding? Will you follow My instructions even when they don't make sense to you?"

3. The Goal: Holiness Has a Divine Purpose

The third truth revealed at Cana is that holiness always has a purpose that goes far beyond the current situation. It has an eternal goal in mind, even while it deals with the circumstances as they are right now.

John tells us the purpose of this miracle in verse 11: "This, the first of his signs, Jesus did at Cana in Galilee, and manifested his glory. And his disciples believed in him" (John 2:11 ESV).

Jesus didn't just solve a hospitality problem. This wasn't just about keeping a family from embarrassment. The goal of the miracle was to manifest His glory and inspire belief in His disciples. The wine shortage was just the occasion, not the ultimate purpose.

We must understand this truth about holiness: When God takes holy action in our lives, He's pointing to something even bigger. God is revealing His glory and strengthening our faith while He meets our immediate needs at the same time.

Think about how much wine Jesus produced. There were six stone jars that held twenty to thirty gallons each! What that means is Jesus created somewhere between 120 and 180 gallons of premium wine. That's between 600 and 900 bottles in modern terms! For a village wedding, this was huge!

Why did Jesus make so much wine? Because He wasn't just helping out a wedding party; He was making a statement about the lavish nature of God's Kingdom. Jesus was showing that when God's holiness breaks into human need, it doesn't provide just enough—it provides abundance beyond imagination.

Notice also what happens at the end of the story. The master of the feast calls the bridegroom and compliments him on saving the best wine for last. The master doesn't have any idea where the wine came from, so he gives the credit to the bridegroom, not to Jesus.

Even the quiet nature of this miracle shows us something profound about holiness: it often works behind the scenes, not seeking credit or applause. Jesus didn't make a big deal of His miracle. He didn't use it as a platform to deliver a speech or a sermon. In fact, He didn't try to attract attention to Himself at all. Jesus just fixed the problem. Meanwhile, the bridegroom got the honor.

> When God's holiness breaks into human need, it doesn't provide just enough—it provides abundance beyond imagination.

Jesus' example challenges our ego-driven motives. We often want others to notice our good deeds. We want them to think we are spiritually mature and our ministry is powerfully effective. But true holiness is content to work behind the scenes as long as God's purposes are accomplished.

The goal of holiness is never about us—our comfort, our reputation, our success. It's always about revealing God's glory and drawing people into a deeper relationship with Him.

Jesus could have used this miracle to pump up His own reputation. He could have leveraged it to boost His following. Instead, He used it to point beyond Himself to His Father and the coming Kingdom.

Think about your own life. When God is working in your life, whether through blessing or trial, He always has a greater purpose than what you can see in the moment. If God sends financial success, it's not just about paying your bills. He is revealing His faithfulness and His provision. When God heals you, it's not just about relieving your physical discomfort; He's demonstrating His power. When God restores your broken relationship, it's not just about your happiness; He's displaying that He is the God who reconciles all people and all things to Himself.

If we reduce God's work in our lives primarily to meeting our personal needs or solving our individual problems, we completely miss His greater goal for holiness in our lives. He wants to transform us into His image so He can show off His glory to a watching world,

Making Your Heart into Holy Space

So far we've taken a look at what holiness means and how Jesus showed it in His own life by following divine timing, using divine methods, and pursuing a divine purpose. But how do we practically respond to this information? How do we make sure our lives line up with God's holiness?

The answer is simple yet profound: we prepare our hearts to be holy spaces for God to make Himself at home.

All through the Old Testament, God commanded His people to set sacred spaces where His holy presence could live among them. First the Tabernacle, then the Temple—these were physical locations set apart (there's that word again—*kadesh*) for encountering God's presence.

But when Jesus came, everything changed. After His Resurrection and Ascension, He sent the Holy Spirit to live not in buildings made by human hands, but in human hearts. Paul asks in 1 Corinthians 6:19, "Do you not know that your body is a temple of the Holy Spirit within you, whom you have from God?" (1 Corinthians 6:19 ESV).

This is turned those earlier believers thinking about God's presence upside down. And it should similarly flip our thinking . God's holy presence now resides within believers. Our hearts are meant to be the Holy of Holies—the most sacred space where God's presence dwells.

So how do we make our hearts holy spaces? Here are *four practical steps:*

1. Recognize What Holiness Isn't

First, we need to clear away some false ideas. Holiness isn't about:

- **Outward appearances.** Jesus condemned the Pharisees as "whitewashed tombs"—clean on the outside but full of death inside (Matthew 23:27 NIV). God isn't impressed by our religious performance or our "Sunday best."

- **Rule-keeping.** While obedience matters, holiness isn't primarily about checking boxes on a spiritual to-do list. It's about having a relationship with a holy God.

- **Separation from "sinners."** Jesus was called a friend of tax collectors and sinners (Matthew 11:19 NIV). True holiness doesn't hide from the world's messy reality—it jumps in to restore and redeem it.

- **Self-righteousness.** Perhaps nothing is further from true holiness than spiritual pride. Remember the tax collector and the Pharisee in Jesus's parable? It was the humble sinner, not the proud religious leader, who went home justified (Luke 18:9–14 NIV).

2. Cultivate Holy Awareness

Once we've cleared away misconceptions, we need to build an awareness that God is always present in our everyday lives. Brother Lawrence, a 17th-century monk, called this "practicing the presence of God." It means living with the constant recognition that God is with us, in us, and for us.

Practically, this means:

Beginning each day by acknowledging God's presence

- Taking "holy pauses" throughout the day to get your heart in tune with His heart

- Recognizing divine appointments and interruptions as opportunities for holy work

- Ending each day by expressing gratitude for how you've seen God's presence throughout the day

For me, this practice has completely transformed how I live each day. I have reminders throughout my day that cause me to say, "Lord, you're here." They help me remember to pause, even if it's just for a few second, and acknowledge that God is here with me so I can realign my heart with Him. These micro-moments have changed how I experience each day.

3. Surrender Your Agenda

If holiness goes beyond our personal goals, then creating sacred space within ourselves means giving up our own plans and preferences to God. This is easier said than done!

Find your "off-limits" areas with God—the parts of life where you resist His guidance. It might be your career path, your money, your relationships, or how you spend your time. These are the things where you're essentially telling God, "You can have everything else, but I'm keeping control of this."

True holiness requires open-handed living—holding everything loosely and saying with Jesus, "Not my will, but yours be done" (Luke 22:42 NIV). This is a daily decision, not a one-time commitment.

Try this simple prayer: "God, show me where I'm still holding on to control instead of giving in to Your holiness." Be ready for real answers and have the strength to act on them.

> True holiness requires open-handed
> living—saying with Jesus,
> "Not my will, but yours be done."

4. Practice Holy Response

Finally, creating sacred space in your heart means learning to respond well to life's ups and downs.

When good things happen, be thankful instead of feeling entitled. When facing challenges, trust instead of complaining. When someone hurts you, forgive instead of holding grudges. When tempted, resist instead of making excuses.

These better responses don't come naturally; they need practice and help from the Holy Spirit. Eventually, they become more automatic as God's goodness changes the shape of your heart.

Something that helps me is spotting my unhealthy default reactions and replacing them with better ones. For example, I normally get defensive when criticized. My better alternative is asking, "What are you teaching me here, God?" By choosing the better response even when I don't feel like it, I'm slowly changing my automatic reactions.

The Transforming Power of Holiness

When we really experience God's holiness and make room for Him in our hearts, everything looks different. We start seeing our situations, relationships, jobs, and the world in a whole new way.

Holiness transforms:

- **Our priorities.** Things that seemed urgent often become less important. Things that seemed unimportant often become central.

- **Our relationships.** We start seeing people as God sees them—not as projects, problems, or tools, but as image-bearers with lasting value.

- **Our work.** Even ordinary tasks become sacred when done for God. The line between "sacred" and "everyday" fades away.

- **Our suffering.** Pain is still real, but it's no longer pointless. God's purposes give even our darkest times the potential for good.

- **Our joy.** Pleasures mean more when seen as gifts from God rather than goals in themselves.

- **Our influence.** Like Moses coming down from Mount Sinai, time spent with God changes us in ways others can't miss.

I'll never forget talking with an agnostic friend years ago. After watching my life for several months, he said, "I don't think I believe in God, but I'm more interested in the God you talk about than what I've understood on my own." When I asked what he meant, he explained, "Your faith feels more real. It's like God is both the highest authority in the universe and your closest friend. That's...compelling."

That's exactly what holiness is: the perfect combination of transcendent otherness and intimate presence. It's what makes the Christian God completely unique among all religious ideas. And it's what our hearts were made to experience.

Holiness in a Broken World

As we finish this chapter, you might be thinking, "This sounds great in theory, but I live in a messy, broken world. How does holiness work in real life?"

That's a fair question. Holiness isn't meant to be just an idea but something we actually live—even in our broken world.

Remember the wedding at Cana? Jesus showed His holiness not in a temple or on a mountain, but at a party where something went wrong. He demonstrated divine timing, methods, and purpose during an ordinary celebration of an everyday life event.

Throughout the gospels, we can see Jesus bringing holiness into messy human situations—touching people with leprosy, eating with sinners, talking with Samaritans, crying at graves, challenging corrupt systems, and ultimately dying a criminal's death on a cross.

Holiness doesn't avoid brokenness; it redeems it. It enters into the mess with transforming power.

This means you don't need to escape your current situation to experience God's holiness. You don't need a monastery or mountain retreat (though quiet reflection helps). God's holiness is available right where you are—in your home, workplace, neighborhood, and relationships.

The invitation is simple but deep: Will you make your heart a sacred place for God right in the middle of your everyday life?

- Will you accept that His timing is perfect even when it doesn't match what you want?

- Will you trust His ways even when they go against what seems like common sense?

- Will you embrace His purposes even when they mean giving up your own plans?

In a world fixated on self-determination and instant gratification, choosing to align your life with God's holiness is a radical act. It's countercultural. It's transformative. And it's exactly what your heart was made for.

As we continue exploring God's attributes, remember that everything else flows from His holiness. His love is a holy love. His grace is a holy grace. His power is a holy power. Understanding holiness gives us the foundation for grasping everything else about who God is and how He works in our lives. As Peter reminds us, we are called to be holy because God is holy (1 Peter 1:16 NIV).

Your journey into God's holiness doesn't end with this chapter. It's just beginning. As you go through your days, start looking for signs of God's holy timing, methods, and purpose in your circumstances. Make it a habit to pause regularly and acknowledge His presence. Give up your agenda for His higher purposes. Respond to life's challenges and blessings with holy awareness.

As you do, you'll discover that His holiness isn't just a theological idea—it's the atmosphere your soul was designed to breathe.

Personal Reflection and Small Group Guide

Chapter 1 Summary

In this chapter, we explored God's holiness as His most essential attribute. Holiness isn't merely moral purity but means God is utterly set apart from all creation—in a category all His own. Through Jesus's first miracle at Cana, we discovered three facets of holy living: divine timing that transcends our schedules, divine methods that often contradict conventional wisdom, and divine purposes that seek God's glory rather than immediate human gratification. True holiness isn't about external appearances or rule-keeping, but about making our hearts sacred space where God's presence can dwell. When we recognize God's holiness, we begin to align our lives with His higher agenda rather than demanding He align with ours.

Key Scripture

"Holy, holy, holy is the LORD of hosts; the whole earth is full of his glory!" (Isaiah 6:3 ESV)

Key Thought

"Holiness doesn't avoid brokenness; it redeems it. It enters into the mess with transforming power."

Personal Reflection

1. When was the last time you had an "Isaiah 6 moment" where you were overwhelmed by God's holiness? How did it change your perspective?

2. In what area of your life have you been most frustrated with God's timing? How does the concept of holiness having a "divine schedule" speak to your situation?

3. Jesus's methods often contradicted conventional wisdom. What is He asking you to do right now that doesn't make logical sense but requires faith?

4. Of the three obstacles to embracing God's methods (love of comfort, desire for self-preservation, need for control), which one most often keeps you from following Him fully?

5. What are your "holy non-negotiables"—areas where you're still resistant to surrendering control to God?

6. How has God's holiness transformed your priorities in the past year? What one priority might need to shift in light of this chapter?

7. What practical step can you take this week to make your heart more of a "holy space" for God to dwell?

Small Group Discussion

1. Read Isaiah 6:1–8 together. What strikes you most about Isaiah's encounter with God's holiness? How might a similar encounter change our church or small group?

2. Pastor Jeff writes that holiness is "the attribute that defines all others." Discuss how God's holiness shapes other attributes like His love, grace, mercy, and power.

3. The story of Cana reveals that holiness has divine timing. Share a story of when God's timing seemed "off" to you initially but proved perfect in retrospect.

4. Jesus often challenged conventional religious wisdom with His higher way. What religious habits or practices might we need to reevaluate in light of true holiness?

5. Discuss this statement: "True holiness doesn't hide from the world; it engages with it redemptively." How can we be holy while still connecting meaningfully with those who don't know Christ?

6. What are some practical ways we can create "holy space" in our daily routines as individuals and as a group?

7. Pray together, asking God to help each person identify one area where they need to surrender their agenda to God's higher purposes this week.

For Group Leaders

Preparation:

Before leading this discussion, spend time reflecting on your own experiences with God's holiness. Be prepared to share authentically about times when God's timing, methods, or purposes have challenged you personally.

Setting the Tone:

This topic can make people uncomfortable if they associate holiness with judgment or perfectionism. Begin by emphasizing that holiness is ultimately about God's unique and separate nature, not primarily about moral rules.

Facilitation Tips:

- For question #2, be sensitive that some in your group may be in the midst of difficult waiting seasons. Emphasize that acknowledging frustration with God's timing isn't lack of faith but honesty.

- For question #5 about engaging redemptively with the world, encourage concrete examples rather than general principles.

- Consider breaking into pairs for personal reflection question #5 about "holy non-negotiables," as this might be too vulnerable for some to share in the large group.

Application Focus:

End your time together by having each person write down one specific action step they'll take this week to align more with God's holiness. This could be related to divine timing (patience), divine methods (obedience in something counterintuitive), or divine purpose (seeking God's glory above personal gain).

2

THE ROCK THAT NEVER MOVES

The Immutability of God

MY MOM'S NAME is Gloria. She had over 50 surgeries before I turned 18. Between my conception until I was 12, she had over 25 surgeries. Every time she had surgery, my brothers, Jimmy and Jason, and I would stay in different houses with friends. Sometimes a surgery along with her recovery would take weeks. When I say we were raised by a community, I really mean it. Our friends and family stepped up when we needed them.

When I was about ten, I became really frustrated with all the disruptions to my life. The summer before, my brothers and I had stayed with a family where we had some terrible things happen to us. I didn't understand then what I know now, but I was deeply troubled by all the different invasions of my heart from some of the places we had to stay. It took me a long time to realize I was carrying a lot of that trauma.

Years later, a mentor was helping me unpack all this emotional history and he asked a very profound question: "Jeff, remember those rooms and houses and all you went through—where was God in those rooms? Pick one. Go there. Where was He?" With that question, I began to see the unchanging, steadfast nature of God's presence in my life.

My mentor revealed something huge in what he said to me that day:

> Do you know what I've learned, Jeff? Almost everything in life shifts. Family shifts. Friends shift. Experiences change. Jobs change. Houses change. But God never does. He's the same yesterday, today, and tomorrow. When everything around you is shifting, He's your Rock.

At first, my young adult brain couldn't fully appreciate this deep truth. But in the decades since, through painful loss, relationship failures, career-ending injuries, marriage challenges, church leadership disappointments, and parenting five headstrong kids, my mind has returned to that conversation over and over.

What my mentor was teaching me about was the immutability of God. This concept is what theologians call God's unchanging nature. It wasn't just an idea to help me pass a theology quiz; it was a lifeline when my world was falling apart.

When everything around you is shifting, God is your Rock.

What Does Immutability Really Mean?

The word "immutable" comes from the Latin word *immutabilis*, which simply means 'unchangeable.' When we talk about God's immutability, we're saying that God doesn't change—not in His essence, character, purposes, or promises.

- Numbers 23:19 puts it this way: "God is not human, that he should lie, not a human being, that he should change his mind. Does he speak and then not act? Does he promise and not fulfill?" (Numbers 23:19 NIV).

- Malachi 3:6 declares it plainly: "I the Lord do not change. So you, the descendants of Jacob, are not destroyed" (Malachi 3:6 NIV).

- And in the New Testament, James describes God as "the Father of the heavenly lights, who does not change like shifting shadows" (James 1:17 NIV).

- Hebrews 13:8 applies this attribute specifically to Jesus: "Jesus Christ is the same yesterday and today and forever" (Hebrews 13:8 NIV).

These verses aren't just dropping random facts about God's identity. They're showing us something absolutely fundamental—while literally everything around us is constantly changing and evolving, God stays exactly the same forever.

> When everything around you is shifting, God is your Rock.

This matters more than you might think. If God could change, our entire faith would be unstable. Think about it: if God's character could flip, how could we actually trust anything He says? If His plans could suddenly shift, how could we feel confident about the future? If His whole nature could transform, how would we ever really know who He is?

God's unchanging nature is the thing that makes everything else in life feel solid. It's the one thing we can count on when everything else is constantly shifting.

Here's the thing: if God could change, He might love you right now but then just ... not tomorrow. He could be fair in one situation but totally unfair in another. He could be loyal to your parents' generation but then ditch yours completely. A god like that would basically be like those unpredictable gods from ancient stories—totally unreliable and actually kind of scary.

But the God we're talking about isn't like that at all. He's completely, beautifully, comfortingly consistent. He never changes, period. And because He's so steady and reliable, it affects everything about how we can relate to Him. We actually know what to expect, and that changes everything.

Three Things God Cannot Do

When we talk about God being omnipotent (all-powerful), we usually say He can do absolutely anything. But that's not exactly right. God can do anything that fits with who He is and what He's like. There are actually some things that God can't do, and it's specifically because He never changes.

Let me break down three of these things that connect directly to His unchanging nature, His immutability.

1. God Cannot Change

The biggest thing about God never changing is that He fundamentally cannot become something other than who He is. His core identity, nature, and character stay exactly the same forever.

This doesn't mean God never moves or that He's boring or predictable. He's fully alive and totally engaged in our world. He hears our prayers, He grieves when we sin, He rejoices when we worship Him. But these reactions aren't Him changing at all—they're His unchanging character responding to whatever we're going through.

Think about how the Bible describes God:

- **He is eternal**—without beginning or end (Psalm 90:2)

- **He is perfect**—complete, lacking nothing (Matthew 5:48)

- **He is self-existent**—dependent on nothing outside Himself (Acts 17:24–25)

If God could change, it would mean He was either becoming more or becoming less. If He got even better (more loving, more just, more wise), that would mean He wasn't perfect before. If He became less, that would mean He's not perfect now. Neither of those makes sense when we're talking about God.

Some people think this makes God seem distant or cold, like He's not really involved. But it's actually the complete opposite. The fact that God doesn't change is what makes Him someone on whom we can actually rely. Because He stays the same, we can build our entire lives around what He says, who He is, and what He promises, without worrying that He's like a fickle adolescent or that He's going to pull the rug out from under us.

I learned how real this truth is during one of the hardest times in my ministry. After spending years building up a church community and really caring about people, everything fell apart because of conflicts and a painful church split. People I had discipled, counseled, and loved just left. Some even spread rumors and told stories that weren't the whole truth. I felt completely betrayed and started questioning everything—whether I was actually called to do this, whether I was any good at it, even who I was as a person.

During one particularly dark afternoon, I was on sabbatical and I was alone in a cabin in Whitefish, Montana. I was surrounded by beauty on the outside but crippling pain on the inside. I didn't see a way forward. Covid shut our gatherings down. Almost every leader serving under me was either attacking me or afraid I wasn't going to make it. All those considerations were somewhat legitimate.

I wish I could say I was praying these deep, spiritual prayers, but I was actually just repeating something my therapist had told me to pray. He said, "Jeff, ask the Lord to show up in a big way while you're wrestling with all this."

So I began to wrestle with Him. It was very emotional. Then a sense of radical obedient trust came over me. I call this a baptism of fire.

It's when the unchanging nature of God overwhelms your whole being—especially your stubborn will.

God spoke to me in my spirit,

"Jeff, has my character changed through any of this?"

I stopped wrestling. "No, Lord."

"Has my love for you diminished?"

"No."

"Have my promises failed?"

"No."

"Have my purposes for your life been thwarted?"

"No."

That moment kicked off a major shift from the cabin to a one-person tent and a 12-day fast where I only drank water. God was pushing me to move to the Hungry Horse Reservoir and live in this tiny tent with just a fire and water, spending time with Him. During those days, He gave me signs that completely overwhelmed me. He showed up in ways I could actually feel and know were real.

I realized I had been doing ministry completely wrong. I was building my whole identity and sense of security on whether people liked me and whether my ministry was successful, instead of basing it on the fact that God never changes. People had changed. My circumstances had totally changed. But God hadn't changed—and never would.

When your whole world is falling apart, this truth becomes much more than just theology or something you learned in church; it becomes what actually keeps you going.

God's unchanging nature isn't some cold, boring church teaching— it's the solid ground that holds you up when everything else collapses.

> God's unchanging nature isn't some cold, boring church teaching—it's the solid ground that holds you up when everything else collapses.

2. God Cannot Lie

The second thing God can't do is lie. This comes straight from the fact that He never changes. Titus 1:2 says that God "does not lie" (Titus 1:2 NIV), and Hebrews 6:18 says it is "impossible for God to lie" (Hebrews 6:18 NIV).

Why can't God lie? Because lying would go completely against His unchanging nature of being truthful and faithful. When you lie, you're intentionally saying something that doesn't match reality. But God literally is the foundation of reality! He spoke everything into existence. His Word actually defines what's true.

Numbers 23:19 connects God's truthfulness directly to the fact that He doesn't change: "God is not human, that he should lie, not a human being, that he should change his mind" (Numbers 23:19 NIV). In other words, humans lie and change their minds all the time because we're unreliable, scared, and messed up. God is none of those things.

Think about why people usually lie:

- To get something they can't get honestly

- To avoid negative consequences of truth

- To manipulate others' perceptions

None of these reasons apply to God. He already owns everything. He's not scared of any consequences. He doesn't need to manipulate what people think about Him because He already knows everyone's heart.

This completely changes how we read the Bible, how we understand God's promises, and how we deal with all the uncertain parts of life.

When we read in Romans 8:28 that "God works all things together for the good of those who love him, who have been called according to his purpose" (Romans 8:28 NIV), we can bank on it—not because our circumstances feel good, but because God cannot lie.

When Jesus says, "I am with you always, to the very end of the age" (Matthew 28:20 NIV), we can face our loneliest moments with confidence—not because we feel His presence, but because God cannot lie.

When the Bible promises that "everyone who calls on the name of the Lord will be saved" (Romans 10:13 NIV), we can be completely sure about our salvation—not because our feelings never change, but because God literally cannot lie.

God has used me to help tons of people work through the same doubts He helped me get through. Doubt and unbelief are far more about emotions and feelings than they are about facts or logic. Most of the time, people feel uncertain because they're focused on their constantly changing feelings instead of God's unchanging promises. I tell them that feelings are terrible foundations but they're great indicators. They show you what's going on inside, but they should never be what you base your confidence in God on.

Your certainty doesn't come from emotions that change all the time—it comes from the solid, unshakeable reality of God's truthful, unchanging character.

3. God Cannot Stop Loving You

The third thing God can't do is stop loving you. This comes directly from His unchanging nature of love.

Jeremiah 31:3 says, "I have loved you with an everlasting love; I have drawn you with unfailing kindness" (NIV). That word "everlasting" is huge. God's love isn't temporary or based on conditions—it's eternal and never changes.

Romans 8:38–39 builds on this:

> For I am convinced that neither death nor life, neither angels nor demons, neither the present nor the future, nor any powers, neither height nor depth, nor anything else in all creation, will be able to separate us from the love of God that is in Christ Jesus our Lord (Romans 8:38–39 NIV).

Look at how complete this promise is. No power, no situation, no dimension, no created thing can separate you from God's love. Why? Because God's love isn't based on things that can change like how well you're doing, how you're feeling, or how faithful you are. It's based on His unchanging character.

This doesn't mean God is okay with everything you do. His unchanging holiness means He always stands against sin. But His unchanging love means He never stops coming after you, even when you're at your absolute worst.

The story of the woman caught in adultery in John 8 perfectly shows this side of God's unchanging nature. When the religious leaders drag this woman to Jesus, they're trying to trap Him in an impossible situation: If He says to kill her, He breaks Roman law and ruins His reputation for being merciful. If He ignores her sin, He goes against Jewish law and loses all credibility.

But Jesus doesn't do either one. Instead, He challenges anyone who's never sinned to throw the first stone. One by one, the accusers walk away. Then Jesus speaks directly to the woman: Then neither do I condemn you... Go now and leave your life of sin" (John 8:11 NIV).

In this moment, we see both God's unchanging holiness—He calls sin exactly what it is—and His unchanging love—He offers mercy when she deserved punishment.

This is so important to understand: God's love for you doesn't go up and down based on how you act. It doesn't get stronger when you're doing well and weaker when you mess up. His feelings about you don't get better when you're being spiritual or worse when you're being lazy about your faith.

Does this mean your choices don't matter? Definitely not! What you do hugely affects how much you actually experience God's love, how effective you are in His work, and what your eternal rewards will be. But your actions don't change the basic truth that God loves you with an unchanging, everlasting love.

When you really get this, it will completely change how you relate to God. You'll stop trying to earn His love and start responding to the love He already has for you. You'll stop being afraid that He's constantly disappointed in you and start believing that He's consistently happy with you—not because of how well you perform, but because of what Jesus did for you.

Look at how John describes it: "This is love: not that we loved God, but that he loved us and sent his Son as an atoning sacrifice for our sins" (1 John 4:10 NIV). God's love came first before you ever loved Him. It started your salvation, and it keeps going no matter how you respond.

What Does Immutability Mean for Your Life?

God's immutability might sound like some complicated theological concept, but it actually has big effects on our everyday lives. Let me share three ways this truth about God should completely change your daily experience.

1. It Provides Security in an Unstable World

We live in a world where things are constantly changing. In just the past year, the world population grew by almost 70 million people. US-China trade is completely shifting. Multiple global conflicts are changing. The Gulf of Mexico is now called The Gulf of America. Technology moves so fast it's hard to keep up. Cultural values that seemed solid completely flip within one generation. The economy goes up and down unpredictably. Political situations change overnight. Even our own bodies change, sometimes in ways we like and often in ways we definitely don't.

With all this constant change happening around us, God's unchanging nature gives us something solid to hold onto. Hebrews 6:19 describes this hope as "firm and secure" (NIV). It's not just wishful thinking or pretending everything's fine—it's actually being confident in God's unchanging character.

I remember going through a major transition in the summer of 2008. I left a ministry I loved in Sulphur Springs, Texas and was learning what real entrepreneurship was all about. I was forced into the tough reality of starting something completely new. We had three small kids at the time. Sarah and the kids moved to Kentucky for the summer to stay with Sarah's parents while I started a new company and slept in my car and on friends' couches for about 90 days.

Keep in mind this was the summer of 2008. Gas prices shot up to $6.00 a gallon. This was the peak of an 18-month recession. This was definitely not the time to start anything from scratch.

I had no idea if or how we were going to make it. My heart was free from caring too much about money. My life was more submitted to God than it had ever been. I had great friends. I was getting regular mentorship. I wasn't doing badly on the inside. But I was running headfirst into God's steady and unchanging nature in a huge way. Everything around me was shifting. But He was not.

This verse really came alive for me: "Keep your lives free from the love of money and be content with what you have, because God has said, 'Never will I leave you; never will I forsake you.' So we say with confidence, 'The Lord is my helper; I will not be afraid. What can mere mortals do to me?'" (Hebrews 13:5–6 NIV).

That summer I started a fundraising and sports marketing company to support our family as we also started a new ministry from scratch. I walked all over East Texas and went into hundreds of high school coaches' offices. God helped me get contracts with over 40 schools to build their fundraising and marketing programs for fall 2008. God's steady love was with me. He went ahead of me but also had my back.

In August 2008, I launched and finished thirteen fundraising events all over East Texas. God showed up! He provided our family with over $80,000 in net profit in the first month. Our family moved into our new home and God re-established our lives and formed new ministry relationships in Rockwall, Texas.

Whatever instability you're dealing with today—whether it's your health, relationships, work, or the world around you—God's unchanging nature offers you the same security. He hasn't changed. He won't change. You can build your life on that truth.

2. It Ensures Reliability of God's Promises

There are 7,487 promises from God to His people throughout the Bible. God's unchanging nature means that every single promise He made is still valid. Unlike human promises, which get broken all the time because circumstances change, people change their minds, or they lose the ability to follow through, God's promises are as secure as His unchanging nature.

2 Corinthians 1:20 tells us, "For no matter how many promises God has made, they are 'Yes' in Christ" (2 Corinthians 1:20 NIV). Every promise God has made gets fulfilled in Jesus, who perfectly shows us God's unchanging character..

Think about some of these promises:

- "My grace is sufficient for you" (2 Corinthians 12:9 NIV)

- "I will never leave you nor forsake you" (Hebrews 13:5 NIV)

- "Surely I am with you always, to the very end of the age" (Matthew 28:20 NIV)

- "I have plans to prosper you and not to harm you, plans to give you hope and a future" (Jeremiah 29:11 NIV)

God's promises aren't just nice sayings or conditional offers. They're unbreakable commitments from an unchanging God.

When you're feeling abandoned, God's promise to be with you hasn't changed. When you're feeling like you're not good enough, God's promise of sufficient grace hasn't changed. When you're feeling like your life has no point, God's promise of good plans hasn't changed.

God's unchanging nature completely transforms how we read Scripture. Every promise becomes solid ground you can build your life on, not just an inspiring quote for your fridge.

> God's promises aren't just nice sayings or conditional offers. They're unbreakable commitments from an unchanging God.

Of course, we need to understand God's promises correctly, knowing their context and how they apply. Not every promise in the Bible was made directly to you personally. But every promise shows us the unchanging character of the God who made it, and that character is completely reliable.

In my own life, I've learned to pray God's promises back to Him—not to remind Him (He doesn't forget!), but to remind myself of His unchanging faithfulness. When anxiety is about to overwhelm me, I pray, "God, You promised that if I give my anxiety to You, You would take care of me (1 Peter 5:7). I'm holding you to that promise—not because I doubt you, but because I trust your unchanging character."

3. It Offers Hope for Personal Transformation

Here's something interesting: God's unchanging nature is actually what makes it possible for us to change. Because God doesn't change, we can.

Let me explain. If God were constantly changing—sometimes loving, sometimes not; sometimes faithful, sometimes not; sometimes powerful, sometimes not—we wouldn't have any solid foundation to grow from. We'd be trying to follow a moving target, never knowing what to expect or how to respond.

But because God is unchanging in His character, purposes, and promises, we can confidently go through the process of being transformed to become more like Him. Romans 12:2 urges us to "be transformed by the renewing of your mind" (Romans 12:2 NIV).

Transformation happens when we line ourselves up more and with the unchanging reality of who God is. It's not about God becoming more like us; it's about us becoming more like Him. And that whole process depends completely on His unchanging nature.

2 Corinthians 3:18 describes this beautifully: "And we all, who with unveiled faces contemplate the Lord's glory, are being transformed into his image with ever-increasing glory, which comes from the Lord, who is the Spirit" (2 Corinthians 3:18 NIV).

Notice the direction of transformation: we're being changed into His image, not the other way around. And this transformation happens as we focus on His glory—His unchanging, perfect character.

This gives me huge hope, both for myself and for others. No matter how stuck we are in bad patterns, no matter how many times we've failed trying to change, the unchanging God specializes in transformation.

I've seen this reality in countless lives, including my own. People who are trapped in addiction finding freedom. Marriages that were headed for divorce getting restored. Bitter, angry hearts softening with forgiveness and grace. These transformations aren't because of human willpower or self-help techniques—they're the natural result of encountering the unchanging God and being changed by that encounter.

Misunderstandings About God's Immutability

Even though the Bible clearly teaches about God's unchanging nature, there are still some common misunderstandings that keep coming up. Let me address three of the most common ones.

Misunderstanding #1: "If God doesn't change, He doesn't respond to prayer."

Some people wrongly think that if God really doesn't change, He must have already decided everything ahead of time, which leaves no room for real interaction with His creation. In this view, prayer just becomes a religious activity where you don't actually expect God to respond.

But this completely misses the point of God's unchanging nature. The fact that God doesn't change doesn't stop Him from responding to His creation—it actually guarantees that His response will be consistent!

God has set up prayer as one of the main ways He works in the world. His unchanging nature means He will always be the kind of God who listens to His people's prayers and responds according to His unchanging character of wisdom, love, and sovereignty over everything.

James 5:16 tells us that "the prayer of a righteous person is powerful and effective" (James 5:16 NIV). This would be a false promise if God's unchanging nature meant He doesn't respond to prayer.

When you pray, you're not trying to change God's character or force Him to do something He doesn't want to do. You're inviting His unchanging character and purposes to show up in your specific situation. Prayer doesn't change God's nature—it lines you up with it and invites it to be expressed in your life.

Misunderstanding #2: "The Bible says God 'relented' or 'changed His mind' in several places, so He must not be immutable."

It's true that the Bible sometimes uses language that suggests God "changed His mind" or "relented" from something He was going to do. For example, after the golden calf incident, Exodus 32:14 says, "Then the Lord relented and did not bring on his people the disaster he had threatened" (Exodus 32:14 NIV).

How do we reconcile this with God's immutability? The answer lies in understanding anthropomorphic language—describing God in human terms to help us grasp aspects of His nature and actions.

When the Bible says God "relented," it's not saying His character or ultimate purposes changed, but describing how His unchanging character responded to changing human circumstances. God always responds to repentance with mercy—not because He changes, but because He doesn't!

His warnings of judgment are always meant to lead people to repentance. When they repent, His unchanging mercy responds accordingly. This isn't God changing His mind—it's God's unchanging character responding consistently to changing human choices.

Think of it this way: The sun doesn't change its nature when it hardens clay and softens wax. The difference isn't in the sun but in the materials being affected. Similarly, God's unchanging nature produces different effects depending on how people respond to Him.

Misunderstanding #3: "If God is immutable, He must be distant and emotionless."

Some people picture the unchanging God as a cold, emotionless being who watches human suffering without feeling anything. Nothing could be more wrong!

The Bible repeatedly describes God experiencing emotions—joy, grief, anger, delight, jealousy. Jesus, who perfectly shows us God's nature, cried at Lazarus's tomb, angrily drove merchants out of the Temple, and felt deep compassion for crowds of people.

God's unchanging nature doesn't mean He has no emotions—it means His emotions are perfectly consistent with His unchanging character. Unlike our emotions, which often control us and change randomly, God's emotions perfectly express His eternal nature.

> God's unchanging nature doesn't mean He has no emotions—it means His emotions are perfectly consistent with His unchanging character.

God's grief over sin isn't an emotional breakdown—it's the consistent response of His unchanging holiness to rebellion. His joy over repentance isn't Him being moody—it's the consistent response of His unchanging mercy to people returning to Him.

The God revealed in the Bible isn't unpredictable with His feelings or distant in how He acts. He's consistently, unchangingly engaged with His creation, responding with perfect emotional integrity to every situation.

Finding Rest in the Unchanging God

So how do we actually apply this understanding of God's unchanging nature to our daily lives? Let me suggest four ways to find rest in the unchanging God.

1. Build Your Identity on Who He Is, Not What's Happening

Most of us build our identity around things that can change—our relationships, achievements, appearance, abilities, or reputation. But all of these can and do change, sometimes dramatically and when we least expect it.

God's unchanging nature invites us to root our identity in something—or rather Someone—who never changes. As Paul writes in Colossians 3:3, "your life is now hidden with Christ in God" (Colossians 3:3 NIV).

When your identity is anchored in Christ, the inevitable changes of life—whether good or bad—don't determine your worth or security. You can celebrate wins without being defined by them. You can get through failures without being destroyed by them. You can face aging, illness, or loss with grace because these changes don't touch the core of who you are in Christ.

Practically, this means regularly reminding yourself of unchanging truths about who God is and who you are in Him. Start your day by declaring these truths. Write them down where you'll see them. Say them out loud when changes threaten to mess with your stability.

2. Evaluate Your Circumstances Through the Lens of His Character

Life is full of confusing, painful, and seemingly pointless circumstances. If we judge God's character based on what's happening to us, we'll end up with a really messed up view of who He is.

Instead, God's unchanging nature invites us to look at our circumstances through the lens of His unchanging character. This doesn't make the pain or confusion go away, but it puts them in proper perspective.

As Joseph told his brothers who had sold him into slavery, "You intended to harm me, but God intended it for good to accomplish what is now being done, the saving of many lives" (Genesis 50:20 NIV). Joseph didn't pretend that the evil things done to him weren't actually bad, but he looked at them through the lens of God's unchanging goodness and ultimate control over everything.

Practically, when you're facing difficult circumstances, ask yourself: "What do I know to be true about God's character that helps me understand this situation? How might His unchanging love, wisdom, and power be working even here?"

3. Make Decisions Based on Eternal Principles, Not Temporal Pressures

In a rapidly changing culture, the pressure to compromise biblical values is intense. What was considered obviously right just one generation ago is now questioned or completely rejected. In this context, God's unchanging nature provides a fixed reference point for making ethical decisions.

As Isaiah 40:8 reminds us, "The grass withers and the flowers fall, but the word of our God endures forever" (NIV). Cultural values change. Popular opinions shift. But God's character—and the principles that flow from it—stay constant.

Practically, this means regularly aligning your decision-making process with God's unchanging Word rather than current cultural trends. Before major decisions, ask: "Does this align with the unchanging character of God as revealed in Scripture? Will this decision look wise from an eternal perspective, not just a temporary one?"

4. Worship Him for Who He Is, Not Just What He Does

Our worship often focuses mainly on what God has done for us— the blessings, interventions, and answered prayers we've experienced. While being grateful for these things is appropriate and important, God's unchanging nature invites us to worship Him first and foremost for who He is, regardless of our changing circumstances.

Job demonstrated this kind of worship when, after losing everything, he declared, "The Lord gave and the Lord has taken away; may the name of the Lord be praised" (Job 1:21 NIV). He worshiped God not because of good circumstances, but despite catastrophic ones.

Practically, make worship a daily priority, especially when circumstances are difficult. Focus your worship not just on thanking God for good things that happened, but on praising Him for His unchanging nature—His holiness, love, faithfulness, wisdom, and power.

As you develop this habit of worship, you'll find that your spiritual stability becomes less dependent on your changing circumstances and more rooted in God's unchanging character.

The Unchanging God in a Changing World

I began this chapter with a story about my mentor helping me understand my experience with so much change and instability as a kid. Let me end with a more recent story that shows the same truth.

Over the years, I've visited multiple aging grandparents in memory care units at nursing homes. They were all diagnosed with dementia or Alzheimer's, and at some point, each could barely recognize family members or remember recent events.

Many times, family members will sit and talk about childhood summers at their house—fishing in the pond out back, helping make their famous chocolate cake, listening to them sing while they worked. They always smile politely, but you can tell these memories mean nothing to them now.

One time, someone started quietly humming "Great Is Thy Faithfulness," an old hymn many remember from church. This classic song about God's unchanging nature and constant love had been one of their favorites for decades.

I was amazed when that person started humming along, their voice getting stronger with each line. By the time they got to the chorus about God's daily mercies, those with fading memories came alive with great conviction. The music and memory were still there.

When the resident finished singing, there were tears in their eyes. "He never changes," they whispered to themselves and everyone around. The miracle was when everyone in the room realized: "Even when we forget everything else, we can remember that."

This shows the power of God's unchanging nature. Even when our loved ones' minds change completely, losing memories that defined their lives, the truth about God's unchanging nature stayed deep in their souls.

That's my hope for you as you finish this chapter. In a world where everything and everyone changes—sometimes slowly, sometimes suddenly—may you find rock-solid security in the God who never changes.

Build your life not on the shaky ground of circumstances, opinions, or feelings, but on the solid foundation of God's unchanging character. Jesus promised, "everyone who hears these words of mine and puts them into practice is like a wise man who built his house on the rock. The rain came down, the streams rose, and the winds blew and beat against that house; yet it did not fall, because it had its foundation on the rock" (Matthew 7:24–25 NIV).

The storms will come. Everything will shift. But the Rock never moves.

Personal Reflection and Small Group Guide

Chapter Summary

This chapter explores God's immutability—His unchanging nature—as revealed through personal experiences of childhood trauma and ministry challenges. Unlike people, circumstances, or cultural values that constantly shift, God remains eternally consistent in His character, purposes, and promises. The chapter examines three things God cannot do because of His immutable nature: He cannot change, He cannot lie, and He cannot stop loving us. Understanding God's unchanging nature provides security in an unstable world, ensures the reliability of His biblical promises, and offers hope for personal transformation. When we anchor our identity in God's unchanging character rather than our shifting circumstances, we discover an unshakable foundation for life—because while everything around us changes, the Rock never moves.

Key Scripture

"Jesus Christ is the same yesterday and today and forever." (Hebrews 13:8 NIV)

Key Thought

"When everything around you is shifting, God is your rock."

Personal Reflection

1. What area of your life is currently experiencing the most upheaval or uncertainty? How might God's unchanging presence in those difficult "rooms and houses" of your experience bring comfort to your current situation?

2. Of the three things God cannot do—change His character, lie, or stop loving you—which one challenges your current doubts or fears the most? Why do you think this particular aspect of His immutability speaks to your heart right now?

3. Out of the 7,487 promises in Scripture, which one do you most need to "bank on" in your current season? How does knowing that God literally cannot lie transform how you receive this promise?

4. In what ways have you been building your identity on shifting foundations (people's approval, career success, family stability) rather than on the Rock that never moves? What would it look like to transfer that foundation?

5. Describe a time when everything around you was "falling apart" but you experienced God's steady presence. How did His unchanging nature become more than just theology during that crisis?

6. When you're tempted to evaluate God's character through your circumstances, what unchanging truth about Him do you need to declare? How might this shift from emotional reasoning to eternal reality change your daily perspective?

7. What is one concrete way you can anchor yourself more deeply in God's immutability this week, especially when your emotions or situations start to overwhelm you?

Small Group Discussion

1. Read Malachi 3:6, Numbers 23:19, and Hebrews 13:8 together. How do these verses address the human tendency to project our changeability onto God? What comfort do they offer?

2. The author states that "if God could change, our entire faith would be unstable." Discuss why God's immutability is the foundation that makes everything else secure. How would Christianity be different if God were as unpredictable as ancient mythological gods?

3. Share about a time when you found yourself judging God's character based on painful circumstances rather than viewing those circumstances through the lens of His unchanging goodness. What helped you make that crucial shift in perspective?

4. The chapter addresses three misunderstandings: that immutability means God doesn't respond to prayer, that biblical language about God "relenting" contradicts His unchanging nature, and that immutability makes God emotionally distant. Which of these have you wrestled with, and how does proper understanding bring clarity?

5. Explore this paradox: "God's unchanging nature is actually what makes it possible for us to change." How has the stability of God's character provided the foundation for transformation in your own life or in someone you know?

6. In our rapidly shifting cultural landscape, how does anchoring yourself in God's unchanging Word help you make decisions based on "eternal principles rather than temporal pressures"? Share a specific example.

7. The author mentions learning to "pray God's promises back to Him—not to remind Him, but to remind myself of His unchanging faithfulness." Share a biblical promise that has served as an anchor during difficult seasons and how God's immutability made that promise more meaningful to you.

For Group Leaders

Preparation:

Before leading this discussion, consider areas in your own life where you've experienced God's unchanging nature during seasons of significant change. Be ready to vulnerably share how God's immutability has been an anchor for your soul. This sets the tone for authentic conversation.

Setting the Tone:

This topic often surfaces deep emotions related to disappointment, abandonment, or betrayal. People may have experienced significant changes in relationships, health, or circumstances that have shaken their faith. Create a safe environment where these struggles can be honestly expressed without quick fixes or spiritual platitudes.

Facilitation Tips:

- For question #3 about judging God's character through circumstances, expect vulnerable sharing about times when pain clouded people's view of God. Validate these honest struggles while gently guiding the group back to how God's unchanging nature reframes even our darkest experiences.

- When discussing cultural shifts and biblical values (question #6), keep the focus on God's immutability as our anchor rather than allowing the conversation to drift into divisive political territory or culture war debates.

- Consider having the group break into pairs for question #7 about praying God's promises back to Him. This allows for more personal sharing about specific promises that have sustained people through difficult seasons.

- For question #2 about the paradox of change, be prepared to help people work through the seeming contradiction. Use examples from the chapter (like the author's ministry crisis) to illustrate how God's stability enables our transformation.

- Have index cards available for people to write down one unchanging truth about God they need to declare over their current circumstances (connecting to personal question #6). These can become prayer focuses for the week ahead.

Application Focus:

End your session by having each person complete this sentence: "Because God never changes, I can trust Him with _____ that is changing in my life." Push for specific, real-life stuff rather than general spiritual answers. Follow up on these in your next meeting to celebrate how God's unchanging nature helped them get through the week's changes.

3

SUPREME RULER

The Sovereignty of God

COVID BLINDSIDED US. We planted Anchor Church in McKinney, TX in September of 2015. A launch team of just three families grew to a congregation of over 1,500 by January 2020. We were meeting in a public middle school performing arts theatre with 600 seats. We bought land in July of 2019 and had invested over $400,000 on architect designs for our first church building. We just finished our first Anchor Conference in January 2020 and were moving into "20/20 Vision" just like every other church in America. 2020 was to be a "New Era". It did not disappoint. From February of 2020 until January of 2022, the "New Era" included the loss of our meeting location for Sunday services and significant church growth from 1,500 to 2,000 people.

This was a crisis for Anchor. We grew desperate for a gathering place on Sunday mornings in a time where social distancing dominated mindsets. Commercial spaces large enough to hold our congregation were closed for worship services. A friend allowed us to gather on Sunday evening's in his church building some of this time, but nothing was the same. Our leadership team spent countless hours viewing unsuitable properties, making desperate phone calls, and praying for a miracle.

One day in late March of 2021, I was taking my 12 yr old daughter, Cassidy, on a daddy-daughter date. We passed up a local church's Easter advertising sign and Cassidy said, "Dad, after our date I want to go to the new property and see the new building."

I was shocked. There was no building. I had given up on the dream of having one. I just talked to the elders about selling the property and pivoting. But something about her statement was prophetic. That statement sparked an impromptu elders' meeting the very next day.

This was just two weeks before Easter of 2021. That statement led us to another determined meeting with our bank president. That meeting led to a lunch with a financing company president. That lunch led to an unexpected sunrise Anchor Easter service with a huge crowd that included the finance company president. That service led to a truly miraculous provision of over $12,000,000 in financing for our first church building.

This past Easter, 2025, we had 4,930 in attendance in our eight live services in our new building. Our elders and I deeply know, "Not one moment of this caught God by surprise."

These words move me deeply to this day. While I'd been in panic mode, God had been in provision mode. While I'd been scrambling for solutions, God had been orchestrating circumstances. While I'd been feeling abandoned, God had been actively working through an entirely different congregation to meet our needs.

I had intellectually believed in God's sovereignty all my life. But in that holy season of multiple divine moments, the theological concept collided with my lived experience, and I understood it in a whole new way.

> While I'd been in panic mode, God had been in provision mode.

What Is Sovereignty?

The sovereignty of God might be the most foundational yet misunderstood attribute of God's character. Simply put, sovereignty means supreme power, authority, and rulership. When we say God is sovereign, we're declaring that He is the ultimate authority over all creation—from the farthest galaxy to the smallest subatomic particle, from world events to the most intimate details of your life.

Scripture repeatedly affirms this truth:

- "The LORD has established his throne in heaven, and his kingdom rules over all" (Psalm 103:19 NIV).

- "Our God is in heaven; he does whatever pleases him" (Psalm 115:3 NIV).

- "I know that you can do all things; no purpose of yours can be thwarted" (Job 42:2 NIV).

- "He does as he pleases with the powers of heaven and the peoples of the earth. No one can hold back his hand or say to him: 'What have you done?'" (Daniel 4:35 NIV).

- In the New Testament, Paul declares that God "works out everything in conformity with the purpose of his will" (Ephesians 1:11 NIV).

These aren't isolated verses; they represent a consistent biblical theme that God reigns supreme over everything that exists. This sovereignty operates on *two important levels:*

First, God reigns over the universe. He is the Creator who spoke all things into existence and holds all things together by His power. Nothing happens in the physical realm that is outside His governance.

Second, and more personally, God reigns over every heart. God has given people real freedom to make choices and be responsible for them. But at the same time, He's still actively working through those choices to accomplish what He wants to do.

This dual control—over the universe and over personal lives—is the foundation for understanding how God relates to everything He created and to each of us personally.

The Feeding of 5,000: Sovereignty on Display

One of the clearest examples of God's control over everything happens when Jesus feeds 5,000 people with just a few loaves and fish. This is the only miracle that all four Gospel included in their accounts.

In John chapter 6, Jesus has a huge crowd following Him because they've seen the miracles He's been doing. When evening comes, the disciples realize they have a problem. There's thousands of hungry people stuck in the middle of nowhere with no food.

Jesus asks Philip, "Where shall we buy bread for these people to eat?" (John 6:5 NIV). John tells us that Jesus "asked this only to test him, for he already had in mind what he was going to do" (John 6:6 NIV).

This small detail shows us something huge about how God operates. Even though Jesus asks Philip what to do, He already has the whole thing figured out. He's not asking because He's confused. Jesus is creating a moment to teach Philip something.

Andrew finds a boy with five small barley loaves and two fish. That's nowhere near enough food for this massive crowd. But when Jesus takes it, this tiny amount becomes more than enough. After thanking God, Jesus feeds everyone there. That's around 5,000 men plus all the women and children. And they still have twelve baskets of leftovers!

This miracle shows us several important things about God's sovereignty:

1. Jesus Had Divine Foreknowledge

Jesus "already had in mind what he was going to do" before He even asked Philip for input. This wasn't Jesus scrambling to figure things out. It was His plan unfolding exactly as He intended. God's sovereignty includes knowing perfectly what's going to happen and what He plans to do about it.

How often do we freak out when we're facing what seems impossible, forgetting that God already knows exactly how He's going to handle it? His sovereignty isn't just about having the power to do something—it's about knowing exactly what needs to be done.

2. Jesus Used Inadequate Resources

The five loaves and two fish were ridiculously insufficient for what they needed. But Jesus intentionally chose to work with what was humanly inadequate to show off God's divine sufficiency.

God's sovereignty often works this way in our lives. He doesn't usually drop perfect solutions from Heaven; He takes our insufficient resources, abilities, and efforts and multiplies them beyond what's naturally possible. As Paul found out, God's power is "made perfect in weakness" (2 Corinthians 12:9 NIV).

3. Jesus Created Abundance from Nothing

The miracle wasn't just about fixing the immediate problem; it was about showing off extravagant provision. Twelve baskets of leftovers remained. That was more than they started with! This shows us a key part of God's sovereignty: He doesn't just barely cover our needs; He works with crazy abundance. The twelve baskets of leftovers wasn't a random number. It was meant to be a sign of sovereignty to each of the twelve disciples and showed God's timeless rulership even over the twelve tribes of Israel and the twelve sons of Jacob.

As the crowd sat down on the green grass to eat their miraculous meal, they were experiencing firsthand what it means to be under the care of the sovereign Psalm 23 Lord, their Shepherd. They were made to lie down in a green pasture. They didn't lack anything. Every detail mattered. When God exercises His supreme authority in our lives, it doesn't result in just getting by but in "life ... to the full" (John 10:10 NIV).

4. Jesus Demonstrated Sovereignty Over Natural Law

Most obviously, Jesus showed His authority over physical reality itself. Matter can't normally be created or multiplied like this, which goes against everything we know about physics. But Jesus, as sovereign Creator, isn't limited by the natural laws. He's the one who set them up in the first place.

We have to understand that God's sovereignty means He works both within natural laws and, when it serves His purposes, beyond them. Miracles aren't God breaking His own rules; they're God exercising His authority as the One who wrote those rules to start with.

Jesus Walking on Water: Another Dimension of Sovereignty

Right after the feeding miracle, John's Gospel records another incredible demonstration of divine sovereignty—Jesus walking on water. After sending the crowd away, Jesus tells His disciples to go ahead of Him in a boat while He goes up a mountain to pray.

As the disciples row across the Sea of Galilee, strong winds create dangerous conditions. Then, in the darkness, they see Jesus walking on the water toward them. Terrified, they think they're seeing a ghost. Jesus calls out, "It is I; don't be afraid" (John 6:20 NIV).

This incident shows us additional dimensions of God's sovereignty:

1. Sovereignty Over the Elements

By walking on water, Jesus demonstrates His authority over the very elements of creation. Water doesn't naturally support human weight, but it supports Jesus because He commands it to do so. As Creator, He has absolute authority over every molecule of His creation.

The disciples had already seen Jesus calm a storm with just a word (Mark 4:35–41). Now they're watching Him treat the turbulent sea like solid ground. Both miracles communicate the same message: nothing in creation is beyond His control.

2. Sovereignty in the Darkness

Notice when this miracle happens—during the night, in the darkness. This matters because darkness in Scripture often represents fear, uncertainty, and evil. By walking confidently through the darkness, Jesus shows that God's sovereignty isn't limited to daytime, good circumstances, or when you can see clearly.

God doesn't lose control when your situation gets dark. His authority doesn't weaken when you can't see where you're going. His sovereignty works just as perfectly in your midnight hour as it does at high noon.

3. Sovereignty Amid the Storm

The disciples weren't just in darkness; they were fighting against strong wind and threatening waves. Yet Jesus walks through the exact same conditions that are causing them distress—completely untroubled.

God's sovereignty doesn't mean He'll always calm your storms, but it does mean He'll always be sovereign over them. Sometimes He calms the storm; sometimes He lets the storm rage while giving you supernatural peace right in the middle of it.

4. Sovereignty That Invites Participation

One detail Matthew adds to this story is fascinating: Peter asks to join Jesus on the water, and Jesus invites him to come (Matthew 14:28–29). For a brief moment, Peter actually experiences the same supernatural ability to walk on water—until he shifts his focus from Jesus to the wind and waves.

This shows us something amazing about God's sovereignty: it's not a controlling power that shuts down human participation; it's a power that invites and lets us participate in the impossible. God's sovereignty doesn't take away human choice; it empowers it.

Three More Things God Cannot Do

In our discussion of God's immutability, we explored three things God can't do because of His unchanging nature. Now let's look at three more things God cannot do because of His sovereignty.

1. God Cannot Lack

Because God is sovereign, He can't experience deficiency or need. Everything that exists belongs to Him and operates under His authority. As the psalmist says: "The earth is the LORD's, and everything in it, the world, and all who live in it" (Psalm 24:1 NIV).

In the feeding of the 5,000, we see this clearly. Jesus wasn't limited by the lack of resources because, as sovereign Lord, all resources already belong to Him. He didn't need to rush to the nearest store; He simply used His creative authority.

In Psalm 50:10–12, God makes this clear: "Every animal of the forest is mine, and the cattle on a thousand hills... If I were hungry I would not tell you, for the world is mine, and all that is in it" (Psalm 50:10–12 NIV).

This changes how we think about our own needs and resources. When you pray for God to provide, you're not asking Him to get something He doesn't have; you're asking Him to give you what He already owns.

I've counseled many people through financial crises who become overwhelmed with a sense of scarcity. I often remind them that while their bank account may be limited, their Father's resources are not. The sovereign God who owns "the cattle on a thousand hills" is not stressing over your mortgage payment or medical bill.

This doesn't mean God will give you everything you want; it means He has everything you need. His distribution of resources is governed by His wisdom, not His limitations.

2. God Cannot Fail

Because God is sovereign, failure is literally impossible for Him. As Isaiah declares: "The LORD Almighty has sworn, 'Surely, as I have planned, so it will be, and as I have purposed, so it will happen'... For the LORD Almighty has purposed, and who can thwart him?" (Isaiah 14:24, 27 NIV).

In both miracle accounts we've looked at, we see this principle at work. Jesus didn't attempt to feed the 5,000; He accomplished it. He didn't try to walk on water; He did it. Divine purposes don't involve trial and error or the possibility of failure.

This doesn't mean everything in your life will work out as you want or expect. From our limited perspective, circumstances often look like failures or setbacks. But from God's sovereign perspective, even apparent failures are serving His unfailing purposes.

Joseph recognized this when he told his brothers who had sold him into slavery: "You intended to harm me, but God intended it for good to accomplish what is now being done, the saving of many lives" (Genesis 50:20 NIV). What looked like a devastating failure from Joseph's perspective was actually God's unfailing plan unfolding.

I experienced this multiple times from 2008 through 2013. I had sensed that God was leading me to plant a church. The first attempt was paused in 2008. Then I stepped up again to launch in late 2010, but one of our children had a near-death medical crisis right when we started the church plant. Sarah was pregnant with our fifth child during the 30-day crisis. All of our advisors asked us to pause the plant again. We did, but I was crushed inside by God's timing delays. I did not want to wait.

> From God's sovereign perspective, even apparent failures are serving His unfailing purposes.

A few months later, I joined the pastoral staff of a very large church. I was grateful but also miserable almost the whole time. I was called to plant a church, not to help a 30,000-member church get bigger. It bothered me. I stepped up to plant a church again, but this time God opened a door for me to become the Executive Lead Pastor of another very large church—with the promise, "If you come help me for two years, I'll help you plant wherever you want to go." Two years later, God moved us to McKinney, Texas to plant Anchor Church.

That's just two paragraphs for you to read, but for me that was eight years of painfully learning God's sovereign timing and process. God's inability to fail means we can trust Him even when we don't understand His methods or timing. Your disappointments, detours, and apparent dead ends aren't evidence that God has failed; they're pathways of sovereign redirection.

3. God Cannot Lose You

Perhaps the most comforting aspect of God's sovereignty is that He cannot lose those who belong to Him. Jesus makes this clear in John 6:37–39: "All those the Father gives me will come to me, and whoever comes to me I will never drive away... And this is the will of him who sent me, that I shall lose none of all those he has given me, but raise them up at the last day" (John 6:37–39 NIV).

Jesus repeats this promise in John 10:27–29: "My sheep listen to my voice; I know them, and they follow me. I give them eternal life, and they shall never perish; no one will snatch them out of my hand. My Father, who has given them to me, is greater than all; no one can snatch them out of my Father's hand" (John 10:27–29 NIV).

This doesn't mean we have no responsibility in our relationship with God. Throughout Scripture, we're called to persevere in faith, to work out our salvation, and to remain in Christ. But these commands are given with the assurance that God's sovereign grip on us is stronger than our grip on Him.

As Paul confidently declares in Romans 8:38–39: "For I am convinced that neither death nor life, neither angels nor demons, neither the present nor the future, nor any powers, neither height nor depth, nor anything else in all creation, will be able to separate us from the love of God that is in Christ Jesus our Lord" (Romans 8:38–39 NIV).

This brings a lot of comfort to those who struggle with doubt or fear about their salvation. Your eternal security doesn't depend on your perfect performance or unwavering faith; it depends on God's sovereign commitment to complete what He has begun in you (Philippians 1:6).

I've counseled believers who are tormented by the fear that they might have committed some unforgivable sin or that they might someday walk away from God. I remind them that while our feelings go up and down and our faith sometimes gets shaky, God's sovereign hold on His children never weakens.

The God who knew you before creation, who called you to Himself, who made you right through Christ, and who is working to make you like His Son will not fail to bring you all the way home. As Jesus declared: "This is the will of him who sent me, that I shall lose none of all those he has given me" (John 6:39 NIV).

Understanding Divine Election Without Getting Stuck

When talking about God's sovereignty, especially regarding salvation, we inevitably hit the concept of divine election—God's choice of individuals for salvation. Few theological topics have caused more debate and division among sincere believers.

Some emphasize God's sovereign choice, pointing to passages like Ephesians 1:4–5: "For he chose us in him before the creation of the world... In love he predestined us for adoption to sonship through Jesus Christ, in accordance with his pleasure and will" (Ephesians 1:4–5 NIV).

Others emphasize human responsibility, highlighting verses like 2 Peter 3:9: "The Lord... is patient with you, not wanting anyone to perish, but everyone to come to repentance" (2 Peter 3:9 NIV).

Rather than getting stuck in theological camps or using complex labels, let me offer a perspective that honors both God's sovereignty and human responsibility:

1. God's Sovereignty in Salvation Is Clearly Taught

Scripture clearly teaches that salvation begins with God's initiative, not ours. Jesus said, "No one can come to me unless the Father who sent me draws them" (John 6:44 NIV). Paul writes that God "chose us in him before the creation of the world" (Ephesians 1:4 NIV).

This divine initiative shouldn't surprise us. Every attribute of God we've explored so far—His holiness, His immutability, and now His sovereignty—points to a God who acts according to His purposes, not in reaction to human decisions.

2. Human Responsibility Is Equally Clear

Just as clearly, Scripture teaches that humans must respond to God's initiative through faith. Jesus consistently called people to "repent and believe" (Mark 1:15 NIV). The apostles urged their hearers to "believe in the Lord Jesus, and you will be saved" (Acts 16:31 NIV).

This isn't a contradiction of God's sovereignty; it's the way God's sovereign purpose is accomplished. God sovereignly works through genuine human choices, not apart from them.

3. The Connection Is Mysterious But Practical

How exactly God's sovereign choice and human responsibility connect is one of the great mysteries of faith. Like the Trinity or the Incarnation, it involves truths that our finite minds struggle to fully understand.

But while the finer points of theology may be mysterious, the practical part is clear: if you're drawn to God, respond! If you've responded, thank God for drawing you! And if you're concerned about others, pray for God to draw them and invite them to respond.

I often use the image of a door to explain this mystery. Above the door is written, "Whosoever will, may come." As you walk through the door of faith, you look back and see written on the other side, "Chosen before the foundation of the world." Both statements are true, operating from different perspectives.

> # If you've responded, thank God for drawing you!

4. Our Focus Should Be Gratitude, Not Argument

The doctrine of election should produce humility and gratitude, not pride or division. Paul didn't present election as a theological puzzle to solve but as a reason for praise: "Praise be to the God and Father of our Lord Jesus Christ, who has blessed us in the heavenly realms with every spiritual blessing in Christ. For he chose us in him before the creation of the world..." (Ephesians 1:3–4 NIV).

If you've experienced God's saving grace, the appropriate response isn't to argue about how it happened but to thank God that it happened. As Jesus told His disciples, "You did not choose me, but I chose you" (John 15:16 NIV). This reality should produce unity and humility rather than division and pride.

Practical Implications of God's Sovereignty

God's sovereignty isn't just a concept to understand; it's a reality to live in. Here are *four practical ways* this should change your daily life.

1. Sovereignty Produces Peace in Chaos

When you truly grasp that God is in control even when circumstances seem chaotic, it changes how you respond to life's uncertainties and challenges.

In Psalm 46, after describing cataclysmic changes—the earth giving way, mountains falling into the sea, nations in uproar, kingdoms falling—the psalmist declares: "The LORD Almighty is with us; the God of Jacob is our fortress" (Psalm 46:7 NIV). This leads to the famous exhortation: "Be still, and know that I am God" (Psalm 46:10 NIV).

The command to "be still" doesn't mean becoming passive or giving up. It means stopping your frantic efforts to control what you can't control and resting in the One who controls all things. It means trading anxiety for trust, panic for peace, and desperation for confidence.

I witnessed this dramatically in a friend diagnosed with advanced cancer in his late forties. The timing seemed terrible. The diagnosis came in the exact same week of his daughter's wedding engagement. While many would have responded with fear and despair, he showed remarkable peace. He's a veteran firefighter but the calm he had was deeper than his professional skill.

When I asked about his calming faith, he said, "Pastor, this diagnosis didn't catch God by surprise. He knows these cancer cells better than the doctors know them. I don't know why He's allowing this, but I know He's in control of it." Four months later, God healed him of stage four cancer in his blood, lungs, and lymph nodes. He's still cancer free two years later.

Faith like this isn't denial or spiritual bypassing; it's the genuine peace that comes from trusting a sovereign God. As Isaiah promises, "You will keep in perfect peace those whose minds are steadfast, because they trust in you" (Isaiah 26:3 NIV).

2. Sovereignty Encourages Bold Prayer

Some people think that if God is sovereign, prayer becomes pointless. "If God's already decided what He's going to do," they reason, "why bother asking?"

But Scripture shows a different perspective. God's sovereignty doesn't make prayer unnecessary; it makes prayer possible. We pray precisely because God has the power to act, the wisdom to know what's best, and the authority to accomplish His will.

Jesus taught His disciples to pray, "Your kingdom come, your will be done, on earth as it is in heaven" (Matthew 6:10 NIV). This is both acknowledging God's sovereignty and asking for it to show up in specific circumstances.

Throughout Scripture, we see people praying boldly because they're confident in God's sovereignty:

- Moses interceded for Israel, appealing to God's sovereign purposes (Exodus 32:11–14)

- Elijah prayed for fire from Heaven, confident in God's sovereign power (1 Kings 18:36–37)

- The early church prayed for boldness, acknowledging God's sovereign control over opposition (Acts 4:24–31)

God's sovereignty doesn't mean He acts without our prayers; it means He has sovereignly chosen to work through our prayers. He incorporates our requests into His plans, making prayer not just a way to get things from God but a way of participating in what He's doing.

3. Sovereignty Motivates Evangelism

Just as with prayer, some mistakenly conclude that if God sovereignly chooses people for salvation, evangelism becomes unnecessary. But again, Scripture presents a different view.

The apostle Paul, who wrote extensively about God's sovereign election, was also history's most zealous evangelist. After declaring that people cannot believe unless they hear the message, and they cannot hear unless someone preaches to them (Romans 10:14–15), Paul devoted his life to proclaiming Christ where He wasn't yet known.

Far from making evangelism unnecessary, God's sovereignty makes it unstoppable. Because God is sovereignly drawing people to Himself, we can share the gospel with confidence that our efforts won't be wasted. As Paul told Timothy, "I endure everything for the sake of the elect, that they too may obtain the salvation that is in Christ Jesus" (2 Timothy 2:10 NIV).

When I was a young pastor, I worried constantly about whether my evangelistic efforts were effective enough. Was I saying the right words? Was I compelling enough? Was my presentation clear enough? These anxieties actually hindered my witness.

As I grew in my understanding of God's sovereignty, I realized that while faithful proclamation was my responsibility, the results were God's domain. This freed me to share Christ more boldly and joyfully, knowing that God was sovereignly at work through my imperfect efforts.

4. Sovereignty Inspires Hopeful Perseverance

Finally, God's sovereignty gives you the foundation for perseverance through difficulty. When you know that nothing happens outside God's control and that He is working all things for your good (Romans 8:28), you can endure hardship with hope.

James encourages believers facing trials to "consider it pure joy" because these testings produce perseverance that leads to maturity (James 1:2–4). This perspective is only possible if you believe God is working through your difficulties, not just leaving you to suffer randomly.

Paul shows this mindset when he writes from prison: "Now I want you to know, brothers and sisters, that what has happened to me has actually served to advance the gospel" (Philippians 1:12 NIV). While others might have seen his imprisonment as a setback, Paul saw it as part of God's plan.

This doesn't mean pretending that suffering isn't painful. It means trusting that your pain isn't purposeless, that God is working through it to accomplish something valuable that couldn't be achieved any other way.

Drawn by the Father, Kept by the Son

As we conclude our exploration of God's sovereignty, let's return to Jesus's words in John 6: "All those the Father gives me will come to me, and whoever comes to me I will never drive away... And this is the will of him who sent me, that I shall lose none of all those he has given me, but raise them up at the last day" (John 6:37–39 NIV).

In this profound statement, Jesus reveals the beautiful synergy between the Father's sovereign choice and the Son's sovereign keeping. The Father draws; the Son receives. The Father gives; the Son keeps. The Father initiates; the Son completes.

This perfect cooperation between Father and Son ensures that your salvation isn't a temporary status but an eternal reality. You weren't just saved on the day you first believed; you're being saved every day as the sovereign Christ keeps you in His care.

This should remove any basis for spiritual insecurity or fear. If you have responded to the Father's drawing by placing your faith in Christ, you are being kept by sovereign power greater than your own strength, greater than your own faith, greater than your own ability to hang on.

As Jude writes:

> To him who is able to keep you from stumbling and to present you
> before his glorious presence without fault and with great joy—to
> the only God our Savior be glory, majesty, power and authority,
> through Jesus Christ our Lord, before all ages, now and forever-
> more! (Jude 24–25 NIV).

The God who sovereignly rules over galaxies and governments is the
same God who sovereignly holds you in the palm of His hand. God
reigns above it all—over the universe and over your heart.

When life feels uncertain, when circumstances seem chaotic, when
your own faith feels fragile, remember: the sovereign God who drew
you by grace is the same sovereign God who keeps you by grace. You
are being held by hands stronger than your grip, loved with a love
deeper than your feelings, and secured by a power greater than your
efforts.

> God reigns above it all—over the
> universe and over your heart.

As the old hymn reminds us, we rest on the unchanging grace of a
sovereign God who reigns supreme over all.

"Supreme Ruler" isn't just a title we give to God; it's the everyday reality in which we live. Every breath you take, every beat of your heart,
every moment of your existence happens within the sovereign care of
the God who knows you, loves you, and holds you secure.

And that's a truth worth building your life upon.

Personal Reflection and Small Group Guide

Chapter Summary

This chapter explores God's sovereignty—His supreme rule and authority over all creation. As sovereign Lord, God reigns above the universe and over every human heart. Through Jesus's miracles of feeding the 5,000 and walking on water, we see divine sovereignty demonstrated in foreknowledge, provision, and authority over natural elements. We examined three more things God cannot do because of His sovereignty: He cannot lack, cannot fail, and cannot lose those who belong to Him. Understanding God's sovereignty brings peace in chaos, encourages bold prayer, motivates confident evangelism, and inspires hopeful perseverance through difficulties. Rather than eliminating human responsibility, God's sovereignty empowers it, working through our choices and actions to accomplish His eternal purposes.

Key Scripture

"The LORD has established his throne in heaven, and his kingdom rules over all." (Psalm 103:19 NIV)

Key Thought

"From our limited perspective, circumstances often look like failures. But from God's sovereign perspective, even apparent failures are serving His unfailing purposes."

Personal Reflection

1. Recall a time when God's sovereignty was clearly displayed in your life through an "impossible" provision or unexpected resolution to a problem. How did this experience affect your view of God?

2. Which aspect of God's sovereignty do you find most comforting: that He cannot lack, cannot fail, or cannot lose you? Why does this particular aspect resonate with you?

3. In what current situation do you need to "be still and know that He is God" (Psalm 46:10)? What practical steps can you take to rest in His sovereignty this week?

4. How has your understanding of prayer been affected by this chapter's teaching on God's sovereignty? What might change about how you pray?

5. Which area of your life do you find it most difficult to trust to God's sovereign control? What fears or past experiences might be contributing to this difficulty?

6. How does the truth that "God's sovereign grip on you is stronger than your grip on Him" address any insecurities you feel about your spiritual journey?

7. Identify one circumstance that currently looks like a failure or disappointment from your perspective. How might God's sovereign purposes be at work even in this situation?

Small Group Discussion

1. Read John 6:1–15 together. What aspects of God's sovereignty do you see displayed in the feeding of the 5,000? How might these aspects apply to challenges your group members are currently facing?

2. Pastor Jeff writes, "God's sovereignty doesn't take away human choice; it empowers it." Discuss how God's control and human responsibility work together rather than opposing each other. How have you experienced this in your own life?

3. Share experiences of how God has worked through "inadequate resources" in your life or ministry—times when He multiplied what seemed insufficient to accomplish something significant.

4. How does God's sovereignty impact evangelism? Does knowing that God sovereignly draws people to Himself make you more or less motivated to share the gospel? Why?

5. Discuss how your group might respond differently to current cultural challenges with a stronger grasp of God's sovereignty. What would change in your reactions to troubling news or societal shifts?

6. Many people misunderstand sovereignty as fatalism ("whatever will be, will be") or God controlling people like puppets. How would you explain the difference between these misconceptions and biblical sovereignty?

7. Read Romans 8:28–39 together. How does this passage connect God's sovereignty to His love and our security? Share specific ways these verses might apply to situations group members are currently facing.

For Group Leaders

Preparation:

Before leading this discussion, reflect on how God's sovereignty has been evident in your own life journey. Prepare a brief (2-3 minute) personal story that illustrates how God worked through what seemed like a "failure" or disappointment to accomplish something unexpected. Your vulnerability will create space for others to share honestly.

Setting the Tone:

This topic can trigger deep theological questions and even painful experiences where people have wondered about God's role in suffering. Establish upfront that questions are welcome, different perspectives will be respected, and the goal is not to "solve" the mystery of sovereignty but to find practical comfort and guidance in it.

Facilitation Tips:

- For question #1 about John 6, consider dividing the group to focus on different aspects (foreknowledge, inadequate resources, abundance, authority over nature) and then share insights.

- When discussing question #4 about evangelism, be sensitive to those who may feel guilty about past evangelistic efforts. Keep the focus on freedom and confidence rather than obligation.

- For question #5 about cultural challenges, avoid letting the discussion become politically divisive. Steer toward biblical principles and personal applications.

- Question #6 about misconceptions may surface hidden theological concerns. Listen carefully to detect underlying issues that might need follow-up conversation outside the group.

Application Focus:

End your time by having each person complete this sentence: "Because God is sovereign, this week I will _____." Encourage specific applications rather than general spiritual statements. These might include resting from anxiety about a situation, boldly sharing faith with someone, persevering through a difficult circumstance, or praying with new confidence for something that seemed impossible. Follow up on these applications in your next meeting.

4

WHEN GOD DOESN'T TAKE CONTROL

Personal Sovereignty

ON NOVEMBER 22, 2004, our son Hayden was born. Later that evening while I was holding him, God reminded me of a family in town whose four-year-old daughter, Star, was dying of cancer. I felt like I needed to go to their house around 9:00 PM and visit them. Her parents call that meeting a miracle. When I knocked on their door, it was an immediate answer to prayer.

But even after a series of miracles, weeks of remission, and a whole city praying and fasting, Star passed away in her parents' arms.

I was there. I had been there for dozens of nights. I sat on their floor, played songs, and sang while playing Star's pink Barbie guitar. After she passed, her dad and I carried her out to the funeral director's vehicle. She was wearing Dora the Explorer pajamas. My 3-year-old daughter, Shelby, had the same pajamas. The funeral service was packed. I preached and then sang Star's favorite song, "I'll Fly Away" while playing her pink Barbie guitar. The whole room was hurting that day.

As I stayed connected with the family over the years, so many more questions kept churning in my mind. This was a child who had done nothing wrong. She had perfect faith. So much potential. She had such a charming and magnetic personality.

Why would God allow this? If God is truly sovereign, which means He's completely in control, why wouldn't He step in? Why wouldn't He heal her? Why wouldn't He take control of these cancer cells that were destroying this child's body and breaking the heart of a city?

These weren't just big theological questions for me. They were deeply personal and painful. And they get at one of the most challenging parts of understanding God's character—what I call "personal sovereignty."

We've already talked about how God is sovereign over all creation, how He reigns supreme with absolute authority. But now we need to wrestle with a deep mystery: Why doesn't this sovereign God always use His control in ways we expect or want? Why doesn't He always prevent suffering, stop evil, or step in during situations that break our hearts?

After wrestling with these questions through my own struggles and walking alongside countless people facing their own faith crises, I've realized that understanding God's personal sovereignty, the way He uses authority while respecting human freedom, is crucial not just for getting our theology right but for keeping our faith. The most important question isn't "Is God in control?" but rather "Why doesn't He always take control?"

The Difference Between Being in Control and Taking Control

In our previous chapter, we established that God is sovereign—He reigns supreme over the universe and over every human heart. Nothing happens outside His governance or beyond His power.

Yet Scripture also clearly teaches that God has given humans real freedom and moral responsibility. He doesn't manipulate people like puppets or override their choices to force them to follow His plan.

To understand this mystery, we need to recognize an important difference: there's a gap between being in control and taking control.

God is always in control, meaning nothing can mess up His ultimate purposes or operate outside His authority. But God doesn't always take control, meaning He doesn't always override human choices or prevent the consequences of those choices.

Consider these biblical examples:

- God was sovereign when Adam and Eve stood in the garden, yet He didn't prevent them from eating the forbidden fruit (Genesis 3:1–6).

- God was sovereign over the brothers who sold Joseph into slavery, yet He allowed their hateful actions to happen (Genesis 37:23–28).

- God was sovereign over Pontius Pilate, yet Pilate ordered Jesus' crucifixion (John 19:10–11).

In each case, God was fully in control of the situation while choosing not to take control of the individuals' decisions. Why? Because He had greater purposes that would be accomplished through (not despite) human freedom.

This difference helps us navigate some of the hardest questions about God's sovereignty:

- If God is sovereign, why is there evil in the world?

- If God is sovereign, why does He allow suffering?

- If God is sovereign, why do my prayers sometimes seem unanswered?

The answer isn't about questioning God's ability to control all things, but about understanding His choice to sometimes not take control in ways we might expect or want.

> God is always in control, meaning nothing
> can mess up His ultimate purposes or
> operate outside His authority.

The Garden of Gethsemane: Jesus Demonstrates Personal Sovereignty

One of the most powerful illustrations of personal sovereignty appears in Jesus' prayer in the Garden of Gethsemane. As He thought about the suffering waiting for Him, Jesus prayed: "Father, if you are willing, take this cup from me; yet not my will, but yours be done" (Luke 22:42 NIV).

This moment reveals something profound about how divine sovereignty works with genuine human experience:

1. Jesus Expressed Authentic Human Desire

Jesus didn't pretend that going to the cross was easy or something He wanted from a human perspective. He genuinely asked to be spared the suffering if possible. This wasn't rebellion; it was honest human emotion in the face of coming pain.

God's sovereignty doesn't require us to deny our human desires or push down our feelings. Jesus, fully God and fully human, showed us that we can bring our real wants and fears before God even while submitting to His sovereign purpose.

2. Jesus Acknowledged the Father's Authority

By saying "if you are willing," Jesus recognized that the decision ultimately rested with the Father. He didn't demand His own way or try to manipulate God into changing the plan. He acknowledged the Father's sovereign right to determine the path forward.

When we pray, this same acknowledgment should underlie our requests. We ask while recognizing God's right to answer according to His sovereign wisdom, not our limited perspective.

3. Jesus Submitted His Will to the Father's

The defining statement of Jesus's prayer—"not my will, but yours be done"—demonstrates the perfect response to God's personal sovereignty. Jesus didn't resign Himself to a fate He couldn't change; He actively aligned His will with the Father's will.

This is critical to understand: submission to God's sovereignty isn't passive resignation; it's active alignment. It's not saying, "Whatever happens, happens," but rather, "I choose Your way over mine."

In the garden, we see divine sovereignty and human responsibility perfectly balanced. The Father had a sovereign plan that included the cross. The Son, exercising human choice within that sovereign framework, aligned His will with the Father's will.

This model of perfect submission while staying authentically human gives us incredible insight into how we should relate to God's personal sovereignty in our own lives.

The Four Types of Doubters

One of the biggest obstacles to trusting God's personal sovereignty is doubt. When God doesn't take control in ways we expect, we often start questioning either His ability or His willingness to act for us.

In the Gospels, we see various types of doubt expressed by the disciples and others. Looking at these different expressions of doubt can help us identify our own patterns of struggle with God's sovereignty.

Let me introduce you to what I call the four types of doubters—four different ways people respond when God doesn't seem to be taking control.

1. The Safety Monster

The first type of doubter is what I call "the safety monster." This person is so consumed with avoiding risk that they miss God's invitation to step out in faith.

We see this pattern clearly in the disciples after Jesus's resurrection. John 20:19 tells us that "the disciples were together, with the doors locked for fear of the Jewish leaders" (John 20:19 NIV). Even after reports of Jesus's resurrection, they stayed behind locked doors, prioritizing safety over investigation.

Safety monsters operate from a core belief that self-protection is more reliable than God's protection. They've developed such detailed systems of security that stepping out in faith feels irrational or even irresponsible.

I've counseled many people who couldn't follow God's leading because they were too invested in their safety nets. Whether refusing a mission opportunity because it seemed dangerous, rejecting a career change because it felt financially risky, or avoiding honest conversations because emotional vulnerability felt too threatening— their excessive need for safety became a barrier to experiencing God's sovereignty in their lives.

When we prioritize safety above all else, we create a cage that God's sovereignty can't penetrate without our cooperation. God seldom overrides our safety mechanisms; instead, He invites us to dismantle them voluntarily as an act of trust.

2. The Panic Attacker

The second type of doubter is "the panic attacker." This person tends to catastrophize, allowing anxiety and fear to overwhelm their confidence in God's sovereignty.

Peter displayed this pattern when Jesus invited him to walk on water. Initially stepping out in faith, Peter began to panic when he saw the wind and waves. Matthew 14:30 tells us, "But when he saw the wind, he was afraid and, beginning to sink, cried out, 'Lord, save me!'" (Matthew 14:30 NIV).

Panic attackers may intellectually believe in God's sovereignty, but their emotional systems haven't caught up with their theology. When circumstances become threatening, their nervous systems flood with fear chemicals that drown out their rational understanding of God's control.

I've experienced this pattern myself. During a particularly challenging season of ministry, I found myself waking up at 3:00 a.m. with anxiety attacks regularly. Despite knowing God was sovereign over our church situation, my body and emotions weren't convinced. I needed both theological truth and practical tools (like proper sleep, exercise, and counseling) to bring my whole being into alignment with what I knew about God's sovereignty.

God's response to panic attackers is beautiful. Notice Jesus didn't rebuke Peter for falling; He immediately reached out His hand and caught him. Jesus then gently addressed the source of Peter's failure: "You of little faith, why did you doubt?" (Matthew 14:31 NIV). The question wasn't punitive but instructive, helping Peter identify what had interfered with his trust.

3. The Overthinker

The third type of doubter is "the overthinker." This person processes everything intellectually, needing to understand before they can trust.

Thomas represents this pattern. When other disciples reported seeing the risen Jesus, Thomas replied, "Unless I see the nail marks in his hands and put my finger where the nails were, and put my hand into his side, I will not believe" (John 20:25 NIV).

Overthinkers need evidence, explanation, and logical consistency before they can fully trust. They struggle with mystery and tension, wanting to resolve all apparent contradictions before proceeding in faith.

Jesus's response to Thomas is instructive. He didn't reject Thomas's need for evidence; He provided it, inviting Thomas to touch His wounds. But Jesus also gently challenged the limitations of Thomas's approach: "Because you have seen me, you have believed; blessed are those who have not seen and yet have believed" (John 20:29 NIV).

I've known many overthinkers in ministry—brilliant people whose intellectual engagement with faith was both their greatest strength and most significant challenge. Their questions were legitimate, their desire for understanding admirable. But sometimes their need to comprehend fully before committing prevented them from experiencing aspects of God's sovereignty that transcend human understanding.

God doesn't bypass our intellects, but He does invite us to recognize their limitations. As Proverbs 3:5 reminds us, we are to "trust in the LORD with all your heart and lean not on your own understanding" (Proverbs 3:5 NIV).

> God doesn't bypass our intellects, but He does invite us to recognize their limitations.

4. The Stubborn Mule

The fourth type of doubter is "the stubborn mule." This person resists God's sovereignty not primarily from fear or intellectual barriers but from sheer willfulness. They simply don't want to give up control.

The rich young ruler in Mark 10:17–22 illustrates this pattern. After asking Jesus about eternal life, he received an answer he didn't like— sell everything, give to the poor, and follow Jesus. Mark tells us, "At this the man's face fell. He went away sad, because he had great wealth" (Mark 10:22 NIV).

This wasn't a safety issue or an intellectual problem; it was a surrender problem. The young man understood Jesus's requirement but was unwilling to comply. His stubbornness prevented him from experiencing the blessing that lay beyond obedience.

I've encountered this stubborn resistance in my own heart more times than I care to admit. When God's sovereign direction doesn't align with my preferences, I find myself inventing theological justifications for my disobedience. It's not that I don't understand what God is asking; it's that I don't want to do it.

God's usual response to stubborn resistance is patient persistence. He continues presenting the same invitation, the same command, the same direction, often through multiple channels, until we either give in or become so hardened that we can no longer hear His voice.

How Jesus Meets Each Type of Doubter

What's remarkable about Jesus is how perfectly He responds to each type of doubter, meeting them exactly where they are while calling them to greater faith. Let's examine how Jesus interacts with each type:

1. For the Safety Monster: He Enters Their Locked Rooms

When the disciples locked themselves away in fear, Jesus didn't demand they come out and find Him. Instead, John 20:19 tells us, "Jesus came and stood among them and said, 'Peace be with you!'" (John 20:19 NIV).

Jesus demonstrated His sovereignty by passing through locked doors—not to frighten them but to show that their safety mechanisms couldn't keep Him out. More importantly, He brought peace, addressing the very anxiety that had driven them into hiding.

For safety monsters today, Jesus does the same. He doesn't usually force us out of our safety zones; He enters them with us, bringing His peace and gradually building our confidence to step out in faith. His goal isn't to eliminate our desire for safety but to transfer the source of our security from self-protection to His sovereignty.

2. For the Panic Attacker: He Calms Both the Storm and the Heart

In Mark 4:35–41, Jesus's disciples panic during a violent storm. After Jesus calms the wind and waves with a word, He asks them, "Why are you so afraid? Do you still have no faith?" (Mark 4:40 NIV).

Notice the sequence: Jesus first addressed the external threat (the storm), then addressed the internal issue (their fear). He demonstrated His sovereignty over natural forces while inviting them to develop sovereignty over their emotional responses.

For panic attackers today, Jesus still works at both levels. He may calm external circumstances, but His deeper work involves developing our internal capacity to remain peaceful even when storms continue to rage around us. As Paul discovered, God's power is "made perfect in weakness" (2 Corinthians 12:9 NIV), including the weakness of our emotional regulation systems.

3. For the Overthinker: He Provides Evidence While Inviting Deeper Faith

As we've seen, Jesus responded to Thomas's intellectual doubts by providing the evidence he requested. "Put your finger here; see my hands. Reach out your hand and put it into my side. Stop doubting and believe" (John 20:27 NIV).

Jesus didn't criticize Thomas for wanting evidence, but He did challenge him to move beyond evidence-based faith to a more mature trust. The goal wasn't to get rid of Thomas's intellectual engagement but to complement it with heart-level trust.

For overthinkers today, Jesus still provides evidence of His reality and reliability—through Scripture, through answered prayer, through changed lives, through the testimony of creation. But He also gently challenges us to recognize when our demand for understanding has become a substitute for trust.

4. For the Stubborn Mule: He States Truth Clearly While Respecting Freedom

In His interaction with the rich young ruler, Jesus clearly stated what was required but didn't force him to comply. Mark 10:21 tells us, "Jesus looked at him and loved him," then gave him the hard truth about what was needed. When the man walked away, Jesus let him go, respecting his freedom to choose.

Jesus demonstrated that His sovereignty never overrides human freedom. He influences through truth and love, not through pressure or manipulation. Even when someone rejects His direction, He continues loving them and leaves the door open for future response.

For stubborn resisters today, Jesus operates the same way. He clearly communicates what He's asking through Scripture, through the Holy Spirit's promptings, through godly counsel, through circumstances.

But He won't force us to comply. He respects our freedom to choose, even when our choices grieve Him.

How Personal Sovereignty Changes Everything

Understanding God's personal sovereignty—the way He exercises authority while respecting human freedom—transforms how we view everything from daily decisions to life's greatest challenges. Let me share *four ways this understanding should reshape your perspective:*

1. It Redefines How We See Unanswered Prayer

When prayers go unanswered or answered differently than we hoped, many people conclude either that God can't help (questioning His sovereignty) or that God doesn't care (questioning His goodness). Both conclusions misunderstand personal sovereignty.

God's decision not to intervene in the way we've requested isn't a limitation of His power or a lack in His love. It's a sovereign choice that factors in human freedom, natural consequences, and long-term purposes beyond our immediate desires.

Jesus Himself experienced what appeared to be unanswered prayer in Gethsemane. His request for the cup of suffering to pass wasn't granted, not because the Father lacked power or love, but because the sovereign plan required the cross for redemption to be accomplished.

Rather than viewing unanswered prayer as divine failure, we should see it as divine wisdom. It is God exercising His sovereignty in ways that respect freedom while accomplishing His ultimate purposes.

2. It Explains Why Evil Exists Without Making God Its Cause

Perhaps the greatest challenge to belief in God's sovereignty is the problem of evil and suffering. If God is all-powerful and all-good, then why does He allow terrible things to happen?

Personal sovereignty provides a framework for understanding this mystery. God has sovereignly chosen to create beings with genuine freedom, knowing this freedom could and would be misused. He allows the consequences of this misuse to unfold while working to redeem them for greater purposes.

This doesn't make God the author of evil. As James 1:13 clarifies, "God cannot be tempted by evil, nor does he tempt anyone" (James 1:13 NIV). God permits evil without approving it, then works through it without being responsible for it.

The ultimate demonstration of this principle is the cross, where the greatest evil (the murder of God's innocent Son) became the means for the greatest good (the salvation of humanity). God didn't cause the evil actions of those who crucified Jesus, but He sovereignly worked through those actions to accomplish redemption.

3. It Balances Responsibility with Dependence

Personal sovereignty helps us navigate the tension between taking responsibility for our lives and depending completely on God.

Some Christians emphasize dependence to the point of passivity: "I'll just wait for God to do everything." Others emphasize responsibility to the point of self-reliance: "It all depends on my efforts."

The truth lies in the dynamic relationship between divine sovereignty and human responsibility. God works sovereignly through our responsible choices, not apart from them. As Paul expresses it, "Work out your salvation with fear and trembling, for it is God who works in you to will and to act in order to fulfill his good purpose" (Philippians 2:12–13 NIV).

In practical terms, this means we pray as if everything depends on God while working as if everything depends on us. We recognize that our efforts matter tremendously while acknowledging that the ultimate outcome rests in God's hands.

> God works sovereignly through
> our responsible choices,
> not apart from them.

4. It Transforms How We Navigate Suffering

Finally, personal sovereignty revolutionizes how we experience suffering. Rather than viewing pain as evidence of God's absence or His indifference, we can recognize it as the context in which His sovereignty often works most powerfully.

Paul discovered this when pleading for relief from his "thorn in the flesh." After asking three times for God to remove it, he received this response: "My grace is sufficient for you, for my power is made perfect in weakness" (2 Corinthians 12:9 NIV).

God's sovereignty wasn't displayed by removing Paul's suffering but by empowering him through it. This led Paul to a revolutionary perspective: "Therefore I will boast all the more gladly about my weaknesses, so that Christ's power may rest on me" (2 Corinthians 12:9 NIV).

When we understand personal sovereignty, suffering becomes not an obstacle to experiencing God's power but often the very context in which that power is most perfectly displayed.

Thomas: When God Calls Your Name

To wrap up our exploration of personal sovereignty, let's return to Thomas—the disciple whose doubt has been immortalized in the phrase "doubting Thomas."

After declaring he wouldn't believe unless he could touch Jesus's wounds, Thomas had to wait a full week before Jesus appeared again. Then, John 20:27 tells us, Jesus said directly to Thomas, "Put your finger here; see my hands. Reach out your hand and put it into my side. Stop doubting and believe" (John 20:27 NIV).

Notice what happened: Jesus knew exactly what Thomas had said during His physical absence. He addressed Thomas's specific objections with precisely the evidence Thomas had demanded. This was a powerful demonstration of divine sovereignty—Jesus knew Thomas's thoughts and words even when not physically present with him.

But Jesus did more than prove His omniscience; Jesus personally engaged with Thomas's doubt. He didn't dismiss it, shame it, or ignore it. He met it head-on with exactly what Thomas needed to move from doubt to faith.

This is personal sovereignty at its most beautiful—God exercising His supreme authority not to override human freedom but to engage with it, inform it, and invite it into alignment with truth.

Thomas's response was immediate and profound: "My Lord and my God!" (John 20:28 NIV). This declaration is one of the strongest affirmations of Jesus's deity in Scripture. And it came from the lips of the most famous doubter in Christian history!

What transformed Thomas from skeptic to worshiper? The personal, sovereign engagement of Jesus with his specific doubts. When Jesus called his name and addressed his exact concerns, Thomas experienced the perfect balance between divine sovereignty and personal attention.

This is what Jesus offers each of us. He knows your name. He knows your doubts. He knows whether they stem from safety concerns, panic tendencies, intellectual questions, or stubborn resistance. And He's willing to meet you exactly where you are while calling you to where He wants you to be.

The same Jesus who passed through locked doors to reach fearful disciples, who stretched out His hand to catch a sinking Peter, who offered His wounds to a questioning Thomas, and who lovingly invited a rich young man to follow Him—this Jesus is sovereignly working in your life, perfectly tailoring His approach to your specific needs and challenges.

He's always in control, even when He doesn't take control in the ways you might expect or want. His sovereignty operates not through force but through persuasion, not through pressure but through love.

And when you hear Him call your name, as Thomas did, the only fitting response is worship: "My Lord and my God!"

Personal Reflection and Small Group Guide

Chapter Summary

This chapter explores the concept of personal sovereignty—how God exercises His supreme authority while still allowing genuine human freedom and choice. We examined the critical difference between God being in control (which He always is) and God taking control (which He doesn't always do). Through Jesus's prayer in Gethsemane, we saw how divine sovereignty and human responsibility perfectly balance. We identified four types of doubters—safety monsters, panic attackers, overthinkers, and stubborn mules—and how Jesus uniquely responds to each type's specific needs. Understanding God's personal sovereignty transforms how we view unanswered prayer, the problem of evil, the balance between responsibility and dependence, and the purpose of suffering. God's sovereign work in our lives respects our freedom while inviting us into alignment with His purposes.

Key Scripture

"Father, if you are willing, take this cup from me; yet not my will, but yours be done." (Luke 22:42 NIV)

Key Thought

"God is always in control—meaning nothing can mess up His ultimate purposes. But God doesn't always take control—meaning He doesn't always override human choices."

Personal Reflection

1. Of the four types of doubters described (safety monster, panic attacker, overthinker, stubborn mule), which pattern do you most often fall into when facing uncertainty about God's sovereignty? What specific situations tend to trigger this response?

2. Think about a time when you asked God to "take control" of a situation, but He seemed not to step in as you expected. Looking back, can you identify ways He might have been working that weren't initially obvious to you?

3. In what current situation are you struggling to trust God's sovereignty? What specific step of faith might God be inviting you to take despite your doubts or fears?

4. Jesus demonstrated perfect submission in Gethsemane while staying authentically human. Where in your life do you need to pray, "Not my will, but yours be done"? What makes this surrender difficult?

5. How has your understanding of unanswered prayer changed after reading this chapter? Is there a specific "unanswered" prayer from your past that you might view differently now?

6. The chapter states, "Submitting to God's sovereignty isn't passive resignation; it's active alignment." What practical difference would this perspective make in how you approach a current challenge?

7. Like Thomas, what evidence of God's faithfulness has He already provided in your life that you need to remember when doubts arise? How might reflecting on past experiences of His sovereignty strengthen your faith today?

Small Group Discussion

1. Read John 20:19–29 together. Discuss how Jesus responded differently to the disciples' fear (locked doors) and to Thomas's doubt. What does this reveal about how Jesus meets different types of doubt in our lives?

2. Jeff writes, "God's decision not to step in the way we've requested isn't a limitation of His power or a lack in His love." Share experiences of when something you initially viewed as God's failure to act ultimately revealed His wisdom working in a different way.

3. Discuss the statement, "God permits evil without approving it, then works through it without being responsible for it." How does this perspective help address the challenging question of why a sovereign God allows suffering?

4. How does understanding personal sovereignty affect evangelism and discipleship? Does God's respect for human freedom change how we should approach sharing our faith with others?

5. The chapter mentions that God's sovereignty "operates not through force but through persuasion, not through pressure but through love." How might this change how we exercise authority in our families, workplaces, or ministries?

6. Share examples of how you've experienced the truth that "suffering becomes not an obstacle to experiencing God's power but often the very context in which that power is most perfectly displayed."

7. What practical difference would it make in our church community if we all embraced the balanced understanding of divine sovereignty and human responsibility described in this chapter?

For Group Leaders

Preparation:

This topic touches on some of the most profound theological questions believers face, particularly around suffering, evil, and God's role in painful circumstances. Before leading this discussion, reflect on your own journey with these questions. Be prepared to share authentically about times when God's sovereignty seemed mysterious or when His choice not to take control felt challenging to your faith.

Setting the Tone:

Begin by acknowledging that this topic involves mystery. We're discussing an infinite God's ways, which will always exceed our finite understanding. Create a safe environment where people can express honest struggles without judgment. Emphasize that questioning is different from unbelief—many biblical heroes (Job, David, Jeremiah, Habakkuk) asked hard questions about God's sovereignty.

Facilitation Tips:

- For question #1 about doubter types, consider having people first identify their primary type privately, then share in pairs before discussing as a full group. This provides safety for more vulnerable sharing.

- When discussing question #3 about evil and suffering, be sensitive to those in your group who may be actively experiencing trauma or grief. Avoid simplistic answers or attempting to "solve" their pain.

- For question #5 about how sovereignty affects authority, help the group make specific applications rather than staying theoretical. This might include parenting approaches, leadership styles, or conflict resolution methods.

- Question #6 about suffering may evoke deep emotions. Allow space for tears and silence. Don't rush to fill uncomfortable moments with words.

Application Focus:

End your time by having each person identify one area where they need to trust God's sovereignty more fully this week. This might be a relationship, a decision, a fear, or a long-term circumstance. Pair people up to pray specifically for each other about these areas, and encourage them to check in with their prayer partner midweek. The goal is not just understanding God's sovereignty intellectually but experiencing its comforting reality in daily life.

5

KNOWN BY NAME

The Omniscience of God

I TELL EACH of my kids they're my favorite. Also, I never lie about it. The word favorite is what you love or enjoy most based on a unique experience or relationship. I don't love any of them more than the others and this is hard to explain. It's easier for me to explain how uniquely I love each of them and there's really no comparison because my love for each one is so unique.

You are God's favorite. There's never been another *you* and never will be. He completely knows you and knows your future completely. He knows how he made you and knows how he limited you in your design. He knows how you think and has more thoughts of you than you can imagine.

He also knows when you're connected with this deep understanding of His personal knowledge of you and living from that place. This is what changes everything: this all-knowing God knows you, person-ally, deeply, completely and loves you perfectly.

As I've made my way through ministry, through marriage, through raising five stubborn children, through church planting and all its challenges, this truth has become an anchor for my soul. God's all-knowing nature isn't just a theological concept—He's a personal reality who knows my name, my needs, my nature, and my next steps before I take them.

> God's a personal reality who knows my
> name, my needs, my nature, and my
> next steps before I take them.

What Does Omniscience Mean?

The word *omniscience* comes from two Latin terms: *omni* meaning 'all' and *scientia* meaning 'knowledge.' Simply put, God's omniscience means He knows everything—past, present, and future, actual and potential, complex and simple. Nothing is hidden from Him; nothing surprises Him; nothing confuses Him.

Scripture says this over and over:

- "Nothing in all creation is hidden from God's sight. Everything is uncovered and laid bare before the eyes of him to whom we must give account" (Hebrews 4:13 NIV).

- "O LORD, you have searched me and you know me. You know when I sit and when I rise; you perceive my thoughts from afar... Before a word is on my tongue you, LORD, know it completely" (Psalm 139:1–4 NIV).

- "He determines the number of the stars and calls them each by name. Great is our Lord and mighty in power; his understanding has no limit" (Psalm 147:4–5 NIV).

- "Are not two sparrows sold for a penny? Yet not one of them will fall to the ground outside your Father's care. And even the very hairs of your head are all numbered" (Matthew 10:29–30 NIV).

These verses reveal different parts of God's perfect knowledge:

- He knows the huge universe, counting and naming every star.

- He knows the tiny details of creation, tracking even falling sparrows.

- He knows our physical bodies down to the number of hairs on our heads.

- He knows our actions—when we sit down and when we stand up.

- He knows our thoughts before we think them.

- He knows our words before we speak them.

This complete knowledge is what theologians call God's omniscience. It's not just that God knows more than we do; it's that His knowledge is totally different from ours. Our knowledge is learned slowly, partly, and often incorrectly. God's knowledge is instant, complete, and perfect.

But here's what transforms this from a scary theological concept to a life-changing truth: God doesn't just know everything in a cold, computer-like way. He knows you personally, intimately, and lovingly.

The Woman at the Well: Perfect Knowledge Meets Perfect Love

One of the most powerful examples of God's all-knowing nature appears in Jesus's encounter with the Samaritan woman in John 4. This story beautifully shows how divine knowledge becomes the foundation for divine relationship.

Jesus, tired from His journey, sits by a well in Samaria. When a woman comes to draw water, He asks her for a drink. She's surprised that a Jewish man would speak to a Samaritan woman, and their conversation quickly moves to spiritual matters.

Then comes the moment that changes everything. Jesus says to her, "Go, call your husband and come back" (John 4:16 NIV).

"I have no husband," she replies.

Jesus says, "You are right when you say you have no husband. The fact is, you have had five husbands, and the man you now have is not your husband. What you have just said is quite true" (John 4:17–18 NIV).

In this brief exchange, Jesus reveals His perfect knowledge of this woman's complicated life story. Without blame or judgment, He simply states the facts of her relational history—information He could not have naturally known.

The woman had five previous husbands and was now living with a man who wasn't her husband. The fact that Jesus didn't tell her to leave her life of sin is a subtle hint that the previous marriages most likely ended because of reasons other than immorality. We do not know but it is very possible that there was some flaw about her, some problem or inability to conceive that may have contributed to her situation.

It is also possible that the man she was living with was a relative or a relative of one of her previous husbands. There is no accusation of adultery, sexual wrongdoing, or sinfulness. All we know is she had five failed marriages and was living in the home of a man.

The woman's response is telling: "Sir, I can see that you are a prophet" (John 4:19 NIV). She recognizes that Jesus's knowledge about her goes beyond normal human ability. But Jesus doesn't stop there.

As their conversation deepens, Jesus reveals Himself as the Messiah, and the woman hurries back to her town, telling everyone: "Come, see a man who told me everything I ever did. Could this be the Messiah?" (John 4:29 NIV).

Notice her description of Jesus: "a man who told me everything I ever did." She experiences His omniscience not as judgment but as recognition—as being truly seen for perhaps the first time in her life.

This story reveals several crucial aspects of God's all-knowing nature:

1. Jesus Knew Her Past Without Condemnation

Jesus knew the Samaritan woman's complicated relationship history, but He didn't use this knowledge to shame her. He simply acknowledged her reality without adding judgment. This is divine omniscience at work. He shows complete knowledge along with complete grace.

Too often, we fear being fully known because we assume knowledge will lead to rejection. But Jesus shows us that God's perfect knowledge is paired with perfect acceptance. He knows the worst about us and loves us anyway.

2. Jesus Knew Her Present Need for Truth

The woman had deep emptiness and she experienced being known by Jesus more deeply than she had ever experienced. Jesus knew exactly what she was seeking and offered her "living water" that would truly satisfy her soul. His knowledge of her present condition became the basis for Him to perfectly meet her greatest needs.

God's omniscience means He understands your current needs better than you do yourself. He sees past the surface symptoms to the root issues. And He offers precisely what will address those deeper needs.

3. Jesus Knew Her Future Potential

Though the woman came to the well as an outcast, Jesus saw her potential as an evangelist. His knowledge encompassed not just who she had been but who she could become. By the end of their encounter, she was boldly testifying about Jesus to the very community that had pushed her away.

God's knowledge of you includes not just your past and present but your future—all you're capable of becoming through His grace. He knows the person you'll be when His work in you is complete.

4. Jesus Knew What Would Convince Her Heart

Finally, Jesus knew exactly what would open this woman's heart to receive His message. For her, it was the experience of being fully known yet fully accepted. Others might need different evidence, but Jesus fit His approach to what would be most effective for her specifically.

This is perhaps the most personal aspect of God's all-knowing nature: He knows exactly what each of us needs to recognize and respond to His love. He doesn't use a one-size-fits-all approach but engages each person according to His perfect knowledge of their heart.

In this one encounter, we see omniscience transformed from an abstract theological concept into the foundation for a life-changing relationship. The woman didn't encounter a database of facts; she met a Savior who knew her completely and loved her completely.

Three Things Jesus Knows About You

Building on the story of the woman at the well, I want to highlight three specific things Jesus knows about you that should completely change how you view yourself and your relationship with Him.

1. You Are a Unique Masterpiece

God knows you at a level more detailed and complete than you can imagine. Psalm 139:13–16 describes it this way:

"For you created my inmost being; you knit me together in my mother's womb. I praise you because I am fearfully and wonderfully made; your works are wonderful, I know that full well. My frame was not hidden from you when I was made in the secret place, when I was woven together in the depths of the earth. Your eyes saw my unformed body; all the days ordained for me were written in your book before one of them came to be" (Psalm 139:13–16 NIV).

This passage reveals that God's knowledge of you begins before your birth. He designed your genetic code, your brain wiring, your physical characteristics, your personality traits, your talents and abilities— everything that makes you uniquely you.

This isn't assembly-line creation; it's artistic craftsmanship. The phrase "knit me together" evokes the image of a skilled artist carefully crafting a one-of-a-kind masterpiece. God didn't just make humans generically; He made you specifically, with intentional design and purpose.

Think about what this means: There has never been anyone exactly like you in all of human history, nor will there ever be. The particular combination of your DNA, experiences, perspectives, talents, and calling is completely unique. You're not a cosmic accident or a mass-produced product; you're a divine original.

I remember working with a young man in our church who had grown up comparing himself to his highly successful father and brother. No matter what he achieved, he felt it was never enough. He was always the "lesser" version in his own family.

One day during a meaningful conversation, I asked him, "Do you think God made a mistake when He created you?" He looked shocked. "No, of course not," he replied. "Do you think he has a type of success for you in mind that is unique for you?" He just nodded yes.

"Then why are you spending your life shaming yourself for not measuring up to a flawed standard?" I asked. "If God specifically designed you with your particular gifts, personality, and calling, isn't rejecting that design essentially telling God He got it wrong in making you?"

That conversation became a turning point. He began to recognize that comparison wasn't just hurting him emotionally. It was rejecting God's intentional, omniscient design for his life.

God's omniscient design means He knows exactly what He created you to be and to do. He knows your purpose, your potential, and the unique contribution only you can make. This knowledge isn't theoretical; it's personal and particular to you.

> You're not a cosmic accident or
> a mass-produced product;
> you're a divine original.

2. You Have a Unique Destiny

Not only does God know how He designed you, but He also knows what He designed you for. Ephesians 2:10 tells us, "For we are God's handiwork, created in Christ Jesus to do good works, which God prepared in advance for us to do" (Ephesians 2:10 NIV).

The word translated 'handiwork' is the Greek term *poiema*, from which we get our English word poem. We are God's poem—His creative expression, crafted with purpose and meaning. And God has prepared specific good works for each of us to accomplish.

This concept appears throughout Scripture. Jeremiah 1:5 records God telling the prophet, "Before I formed you in the womb I knew you, before you were born I set you apart; I appointed you as a prophet to the nations" (Jeremiah 1:5 NIV).

Similarly, when God called Paul, He said, "This man is my chosen instrument to proclaim my name to the Gentiles and their kings and to the people of Israel" (Acts 9:15 NIV).

God's all-knowing nature includes perfect knowledge of the unique contribution each person is designed to make. He knows your calling before you discover it, your purpose before you fulfill it, and your potential before you realize it.

In the case of the Samaritan woman, Jesus knew she would become an evangelist to her community long before she had any idea of this role. His omniscience concerning her destiny informed His interaction with her.

I've seen this reality play out countless times in ministry. People who thought they were defined by their failures discover God had written a different story for them, one that often uses their deepest wounds as the foundation for their greatest ministry.

Your past mistakes, your current struggles, even your failures don't surprise God or derail His purposes for you. He knew them all in advance and has woven them into His plan for your life. Nothing about your story catches Him off guard or requires Him to come up with a "Plan B."

3. You Need to Be Known

The third thing Jesus knows about you is perhaps the most profound: He knows your deep need to be known. Humans are created for relationship, and genuine relationship requires being truly known and truly loved.

This basic need explains why the Samaritan woman responded so powerfully to Jesus's knowledge of her. After a lifetime of hiding, being truly seen—and accepted despite being seen—was transformative.

The same thing happens in Nathanael's encounter with Jesus in John chapter 1. When Jesus says, "I saw you while you were still under the fig tree before Philip called you," Nathanael immediately declares, "Rabbi, you are the Son of God; you are the king of Israel" (John 1:48–49 NIV). Being known at this supernatural level convinced Nathanael of Jesus's divinity.

This need to be known explains why superficial relationships leave us unsatisfied, why we long for people who "get us," and why being misunderstood is so painful. We're designed to be known—fully, deeply, accurately known—and loved in that full knowledge.

Yet this very need creates a problem within us. We long to be known, but we fear being known, because we worry that full knowledge will lead to rejection. We develop sophisticated ways to hide parts of ourselves we deem unacceptable, presenting carefully curated versions of our lives to others.

God's all-knowing nature cuts through this problem. He already knows everything about you—the good, the bad, the ugly, the secret, the shameful—and He loves you completely. As Romans 5:8 reminds us, "But God demonstrates his own love for us in this: While we were still sinners, Christ died for us" (Romans 5:8 NIV).

The freedom that comes from being fully known yet fully loved is what many people experienced in Jesus's presence. It's what the Samaritan woman experienced at the well. It's what Zacchaeus experienced when Jesus called him by name. It's what Peter experienced after his denial when Jesus restored him with the simple question, "Do you love me?"

This is the amazing gift of God's omniscience: the God who knows you completely loves you completely. And in the safety of that knowing-and-loving presence, you can finally stop hiding and start healing.

Overcoming Skepticism About Being Known

Despite the comfort God's omniscience should bring, many people struggle to embrace this truth personally. Let me address four common sources of doubt and how to overcome them.

1. Shame: "If God Really Knew Me, He Wouldn't Love Me"

Perhaps the most common barrier to experiencing God's omniscience as good news is shame. Many people secretly believe that if God really knew all their thoughts, desires, fantasies, and failures, He couldn't possibly love them.

This shame-based thinking creates a terrible cycle: the people who most need to experience being fully known yet fully loved are the ones most resistant to allowing themselves to be known.

The biblical response to shame isn't trying harder or hiding better— it's vulnerability with the God who already knows you completely. As 1 John 3:20 reassures us, "If our hearts condemn us, we know that God is greater than our hearts, and he knows everything" (1 John 3:20 NIV).

Notice the unexpected comfort here: God's knowing everything is presented as reassurance, not as threat. When our hearts condemn us—when shame tells us we're unlovable—the remedy is remembering that God's knowledge of us is more complete and more gracious than our self-condemnation.

I've counseled many people trapped in cycles of addiction who resist being honest with God because they're ashamed of their repeated failures. I often remind them that honesty with God isn't informing Him of anything He doesn't already know; it's aligning their view of themselves with His view of them. God already knows the full extent of their struggle, and His love hasn't diminished.

2. Pain: "If God Knows Everything, Why Doesn't He Prevent Suffering?"

A second source of skepticism concerns suffering. If God knows everything—including the future—why doesn't He prevent tragedies, abuses, diseases, and disasters? This is perhaps the oldest and most persistent objection to God's omniscience.

This question deserves more space than we can give it here, but a few perspectives may help:

First, God's omniscience operates within His commitment to human freedom. He knows what people will freely choose, but knowing these choices doesn't mean He always prevents them. As we discussed in our chapter on personal sovereignty, God often allows the consequences of human choices to unfold while working redemptively through them.

Second, God's omniscience includes knowledge of both what does happen and what would have happened under different circumstances. He may allow certain painful events because He knows that preventing them would lead to even greater pain or loss of greater good in ways we cannot see.

Finally, God's omniscience means He knows the end from the beginning. He sees how present suffering connects to future redemption in ways our limited perspective can't grasp. As Joseph told his brothers who had sold him into slavery, "You intended to harm me, but God intended it for good" (Genesis 50:20 NIV).

While these perspectives don't eliminate the emotional challenge of suffering, they do suggest that God's seeming inaction isn't due to ignorance or indifference, but to knowledge and purposes that go beyond our understanding.

3. Neglect: "I've Felt Overlooked My Whole Life"

A third barrier to embracing God's omniscience is the experience of feeling consistently overlooked or forgotten. People who have been repeatedly neglected by parents, peers, partners, or society often struggle to believe that God notices them when humans have failed to.

Jesus directly addresses this concern in Matthew 10:29–31: "Are not two sparrows sold for a penny? Yet not one of them will fall to the ground outside your Father's care. And even the very hairs of your head are all numbered. So don't be afraid; you are worth more than many sparrows" (Matthew 10:29–31 NIV).

The logic is powerful: if God attends to seemingly insignificant creatures like sparrows, how much more does He attend to you—His image-bearer, His child, the object of His redemptive love?

Throughout the Gospels, Jesus demonstrates special attention to those society overlooked—women, children, the poor, the sick, the marginalized. In doing so, He wasn't introducing a new divine policy but revealing God's consistent character. God has always noticed those others have ignored.

If you've felt consistently overlooked or forgotten by people, the remedy isn't assuming God is the same, but recognizing that He is different. Humans see partially and value conditionally. God sees completely and values inherently. Your value to Him doesn't depend on others recognizing your worth; it's intrinsic to who He created you to be.

> God has always noticed
> those others have ignored.

4. Self-Deception: "I Don't Want to Be Known"

A final source of resistance is more subtle: some people don't want to be fully known because they're invested in self-deception. They've built narratives about themselves that help them avoid uncomfortable truths, maintain self-image, or justify problematic behaviors.

For these individuals, God's all-knowing nature feels threatening because it challenges their preferred self-perception. As Jesus told the

Pharisees, "You are the ones who justify yourselves in the eyes of others, but God knows your hearts" (Luke 16:15 NIV).

The reality of divine omniscience means we can't successfully hide from truth about ourselves. As Hebrews 4:13 states, "Nothing in all creation is hidden from God's sight. Everything is uncovered and laid bare before the eyes of him to whom we must give account" (Hebrews 4:13 NIV).

This can feel threatening, but it's actually liberating. Living in self-deception creates internal conflict and relational dysfunction. Being fully known—and accepting what God already knows about us—is the pathway to integrity and wholeness.

I've worked with many people who resisted acknowledging certain truths about themselves—their motivations, their patterns, their unresolved issues—until they realized that God already knew these things and loved them anyway. That realization created safety to stop pretending and start healing.

The Benefits of Being Known by God

As we move beyond skepticism and doubt and embrace the reality of God's omniscience, we discover several life-changing benefits. Here are *three of the most significant:*

1. Emotional Freedom

When you truly believe that God knows everything about you and loves you completely, it produces a profound emotional freedom. You no longer need to pretend to be something you're not. You don't have to maintain a performance to earn acceptance. You can stop exhausting yourself trying to appear better, smarter, holier, or more together than you actually are.

This freedom extends beyond your relationship with God to your relationships with others. When your sense of worth and acceptance is anchored in being fully known and fully loved by God, you become less dependent on others' approval and less devastated by their criticism.

You can enter relationships offering authenticity rather than performance. You can acknowledge mistakes without shame spirals. You can receive feedback without identity crises. You can disagree without feeling threatened. All because your core need to be known and loved is being met by God.

I've seen this transformation in countless lives—people who moved from exhausting perfectionism to refreshing authenticity, from defensive self-protection to vulnerable connection, from performance-based worth to grace-based identity.

2. Relational Healing

God's omniscience also lays the foundation for genuine relational healing. Many relationship problems stem from feeling unseen, unheard, or misunderstood. We long for others to truly know us, yet we fear being truly known.

When you experience being fully known and fully loved by God, it changes how you approach human relationships. You can risk greater honesty because your worth isn't dependent on others' responses. You can extend grace more readily because you've experienced grace in your own brokenness. You can listen more attentively because you're not constantly preoccupied with being misunderstood.

I've counseled many couples who transformed their marriages once they grasped this truth. Instead of demanding that their spouse perfectly understand and affirm them—an impossible standard—they brought their deepest need to be known to God. This freed their relationship from an unsustainable burden and allowed them to love each other from fullness rather than desperation.

> When you experience being fully known
> and fully loved by God, it changes how
> you approach human relationships.

3. Spiritual Confidence

Finally, being known by God produces a unique spiritual confidence. Not arrogance or self-sufficiency, but a quiet assurance that your relationship with God is secure regardless of your performance or circumstances.

Romans 8:26–27 beautifully illustrates this: "In the same way, the Spirit helps us in our weakness. We do not know what we ought to pray for, but the Spirit himself intercedes for us through wordless groans. And he who searches our hearts knows the mind of the Spirit, because the Spirit intercedes for God's people in accordance with the will of God" (Romans 8:26–27 NIV).

Even when we don't know how to pray, God knows what we need. Even when we can't articulate our deepest longings, God understands them. Even when we're confused about our own motivations, God sees them clearly. This knowledge provides confidence that our relationship with God doesn't depend on our perfect understanding or flawless execution, but on His perfect knowledge and flawless love.

This confidence transforms how we approach spiritual disciplines, service, witnessing, and every other aspect of Christian life. We're no longer trying to earn what we already have; we're expressing gratitude for what can't be lost. We're not working for acceptance; we're working from acceptance. We're not proving our worth; we're living out our already-established value.

Finding Rest in Being Known

As we conclude our exploration of God's omniscience, I want to focus on the profound rest that comes from being fully known and fully loved.

In our hyperconnected yet deeply disconnected world, many people experience what I call "relational exhaustion." They're constantly managing impressions, curating images, protecting vulnerabilities, and navigating the gap between who they present themselves to be and who they fear they really are. This creates a bone-deep weariness that no amount of physical rest can heal.

Jesus's invitation in Matthew 11:28–30 speaks directly to this condition: "Come to me, all you who are weary and burdened, and I will give you rest. Take my yoke upon you and learn from me, for I am gentle and humble in heart, and you will find rest for your souls. For my yoke is easy and my burden is light" (Matthew 11:28–30 NIV).

The rest Jesus offers isn't just physical relaxation but soul-level peace that comes from being fully known and fully accepted. It's the rest that comes when you no longer have to pretend, perform, or protect your image. It's the rest of being authentic with the God who already knows everything about you and loves you anyway.

This reminds me of a time when my oldest daughter was going through a particularly difficult season in middle school. The social pressures, academic challenges, and her own developmental changes had created a perfect storm of stress. She was trying so hard to be what everyone wanted her to be—her teachers, her friends, even her parents.

One night, I found her crying in her room. As we talked, she finally admitted, "Dad, I'm so tired of trying to be perfect for everyone. I feel like nobody really knows me."

I held her and simply said, "God knows the real you—every thought, every fear, every dream—and He loves that real you perfectly. You don't have to perform for Him."

That simple truth became a lifeline for her during that time. Whenever the pressure to perform would build, we'd remind each other, "God knows the real you and loves that person completely."

This is the invitation God's omniscience extends to each of us: to stop hiding, stop pretending, stop performing, and start resting in being fully known and fully loved by the God who created us, redeemed us, and calls us by name.

As the prophet Isaiah reminds us: "But now, this is what the LORD says—he who created you, Jacob, he who formed you, Israel: 'Do not fear, for I have redeemed you; I have summoned you by name; you are mine'" (Isaiah 43:1 NIV).

The all-knowing God knows your name. He knows your story. He knows your struggles and your strengths, your failures, and your potential, your past and your future. And in that perfect knowledge, He offers perfect love.

There is no greater rest than being fully known and fully loved. This is the gift of God's omniscience to you.

Personal Reflection and Small Group Guide

Chapter Summary

This chapter explores God's omniscience—His perfect knowledge of all things, including the intimate details of our lives. Through Jesus's encounter with the Samaritan woman at the well, we see how divine knowledge becomes the foundation for transformative relationship. God knows us as unique masterpieces, with specific destinies and a fundamental need to be known. Despite common barriers to embracing God's omniscience—shame, pain, neglect, and self-deception—experiencing the reality of being fully known yet fully loved brings emotional freedom, relational healing, and spiritual confidence. Rather than finding God's all-knowing nature threatening, we can discover profound rest in being completely known and completely loved by our Creator.

Key Scripture

"O Lord, you have searched me and you know me. You know when I sit and when I rise; you perceive my thoughts from afar... Before a word is on my tongue you, Lord, know it completely." (Psalm 139:1–4 NIV)

Key Thought

"The amazing gift of God's omniscience: the God who knows you completely loves you completely."

Personal Reflection

1. When have you experienced being truly "seen" by another person? How did that experience affect you, and what might it reveal about your need to be known by God?

2. Which aspect of God's knowledge of you do you find most comforting: that He knows your past without judgment, your present needs perfectly, or your future potential completely? Why?

3. Of the four barriers to embracing God's all-knowing nature (shame, pain, neglect, self-deception), which one most often prevents you from resting in being known by God?

4. In what areas of your life might you be resisting God's complete knowledge of you? What would change if you fully opened these areas to His loving gaze?

5. How does the truth that God designed you as a "unique masterpiece" challenge the ways you compare yourself to others or doubt your value?

6. Where in your life do you most need the emotional freedom that comes from being fully known yet fully loved? What specific behaviors or thought patterns would change?

7. Consider Psalm 139:23–24: "Search me, God, and know my heart... See if there is any hurtful way in me, and lead me in the way everlasting." How would regularly praying this prayer change your relationship with God?

Small Group Discussion

1. Read John 4:1–30 together. What specifically about Jesus's knowledge of the Samaritan woman's life was transformative for her? How does this story challenge our assumptions about what happens when God truly knows us?

2. Jeff writes, "We long to be known, but we fear being known, because we worry that full knowledge will lead to rejection." Discuss how this paradox plays out in your relationships with others and with God.

3. How does God's omniscience change how we approach confession of sin? If God already knows everything about us, what purpose does confession serve?

4. Share experiences of how God has demonstrated His intimate knowledge of you through a "divine coincidence," a perfectly timed word from Scripture, or another means that felt personally tailored to your situation.

5. How might our churches better reflect God's knowing-and-loving presence? What practices could help people experience being fully known yet fully accepted in our community?

6. Discuss the statement: "You weren't created to be a lesser version of someone else; you were created to be the best version of yourself." How does God's omniscient design of each person challenge comparative thinking in our lives?

7. Read 1 Corinthians 13:12 together: "Now I know in part; then I shall know fully, even as I am fully known." What does this verse suggest about our ultimate destiny and our relationship with God in eternity?

For Group Leaders

Preparation:

This topic touches deeply on personal identity, value, and acceptance—areas where many people carry hidden wounds. Before leading this discussion, spend time reflecting on your own journey of experiencing God's knowledge of you. Be prepared to share vulnerably (but appropriately) about a time when you felt deeply known by God and how that experience affected you.

Setting the Tone:

Begin by acknowledging that while God's omniscience might initially feel threatening, it is ultimately the foundation for our most profound experiences of acceptance and love. Create an atmosphere where people feel safe to be honest about their struggles with being known without fear of judgment or quick fixes.

Facilitation Tips:

- For question #1 about the Samaritan woman, consider having the group identify all the ways Jesus demonstrated knowledge of her before discussing the impact. This helps establish the textual foundation before moving to application.

- Question #2 about the paradox of wanting to be known while fearing it may surface deep emotions. Allow space for these feelings without rushing to resolve the tension.

- For question #3 about confession, guide the discussion toward how confession benefits us rather than informing God of something He doesn't know.

- When discussing question #6 about comparative thinking, be sensitive to those who have experienced significant criticism or devaluing of their unique gifts.

Application Focus:

End your time together by having each person complete this sentence: "Because God knows me completely and loves me completely, this week I will…" Encourage specific, actionable responses that move beyond general spiritual statements. Examples might include letting go of a facade in a particular relationship, confessing an area of self-deception, or practicing a specific form of rest based on being fully known. Follow up on these commitments at your next gathering to celebrate how God's omniscience is transforming daily life.

6

NEVER ALONE

The Omnipresence of God

RECENTLY, I HAD the chance to visit Yellowstone National Park with my son. One of the most amazing features in Yellowstone is the Grand Prismatic Spring. It's a massive hot spring with vibrant colors ranging from deep blue in the center to orange and red around the edges.

As we stood on the viewing platform, watching steam rise from the spring's surface, I explained to my son how the different colors are created by various heat-loving bacteria that thrive at specific temperatures. The further from the superheated center, the cooler the water becomes, allowing different microorganisms to flourish in different temperature zones.

What struck me most wasn't just the beauty of the spring, but how constant it was. Day and night, season after season, year after year, the spring remains—steadily bubbling, consistently colored, reliably present. Nearby is Old Faithful, the famous geyser that erupts with such predictable regularity that park rangers can forecast its next eruption with 90% accuracy.

In that moment, I saw a profound picture of God's omnipresence— His constant, reliable, always-present nature. Like the sun that faithfully rises each morning, like gravity that never takes a day off, God's presence is the most dependable reality in the universe.

Yet God's omnipresence goes infinitely beyond natural constants. It's not just that God is always there; it's that He's everywhere at the same time. As the psalmist discovered: "Where can I go from your Spirit? Where can I flee from your presence? If I go up to the heavens, you are there; if I make my bed in the depths, you are there" (Psalm 139:7–8 NIV).

This divine attribute—God's omnipresence—might be the most comforting yet challenging aspect of His nature to grasp. It means that God isn't just watching from a distance; He's actively present in every molecule of creation, every moment of time, every circumstance of your life. Never absent. Never distant. Never unavailable.

> It's not just that God is always there; it's that He's everywhere at the same time.

What Does Omnipresence Mean?

When we talk about God's omnipresence, we're saying that God is present everywhere at all times. Unlike humans, who are limited to one location at any given moment, God exists fully and equally in all places at the same time.

Scripture says this over and over:

- "'Am I only a God nearby,' declares the LORD, 'and not a God far away? Who can hide in secret places so that I cannot see them?' declares the LORD. 'Do not I fill heaven and earth?' declares the LORD" (Jeremiah 23:23–24 NIV).

- "The eyes of the LORD are everywhere, keeping watch on the wicked and the good" (Proverbs 15:3 NIV).

- "For in him we live and move and have our being" (Acts 17:28 NIV).

- When Solomon dedicated the Temple, he recognized the mystery of God being everywhere: "But will God really dwell on earth? The heavens, even the highest heaven, cannot contain you. How much less this temple I have built!" (1 Kings 8:27 NIV).

These passages reveal different parts of God's omnipresence:

- **He is transcendent**—above and beyond the universe He created.

- **He is immanent**—closely present within every part of creation.

- **He is personal**—not just present as an impersonal force, but as a conscious, active Being.

God's being everywhere doesn't mean He's spread thin throughout the universe, with just a part of Him here and a part there. He's fully present everywhere. His presence in this room isn't diminished because He's also present on the other side of the world or in the furthest galaxy. He's wholly present at every point in the universe simultaneously.

This is hard for us to grasp because it's so different from our experience. We're bound by physical limitations—we can only be in one place at one time. Even our digital "presence" through technology is merely a representation, not our actual presence. But God's presence is real, full, and complete wherever He is—which is everywhere.

Three Levels of God's Presence

While God is everywhere by nature, Scripture reveals that He shows His presence in different ways and for different purposes. Understanding these differences helps us navigate the seeming contradiction of seeking a God who is already everywhere.

1. God's Universal Presence

The first level is God's universal presence—His existence in and through all creation. This is the most basic aspect of divine omnipresence. God is present everywhere simply because He exists everywhere.

Psalm 139 beautifully describes this universal presence: "If I go up to the heavens, you are there; if I make my bed in the depths, you are there. If I rise on the wings of the dawn, if I settle on the far side of the sea, even there your hand will guide me, your right hand will hold me fast" (Psalm 139:8–10 NIV).

This universal presence means there's nowhere in the universe where God is absent. Whether in the heights of Heaven, the depths of the sea, or the furthest reaches of space—God is there. Not just aware from a distance, but actively present.

This universal presence holds together the very fabric of reality. As Colossians 1:17 states, "in him all things hold together" (Colossians 1:17 NIV). Without God's active, sustaining presence, the universe itself would fall apart.

In this sense, God's omnipresence is both a comfort and a challenge. We can never escape His presence—which means we can never be truly alone, but also that we can never hide from Him. As Hebrews 4:13 reminds us, "Nothing in all creation is hidden from God's sight. Everything is uncovered and laid bare before the eyes of him to whom we must give account" (Hebrews 4:13 NIV).

2. God's Indwelling Presence

The second level is God's indwelling presence—His special presence within believers through the Holy Spirit. This is a more intimate form of divine presence, available only to those who have placed their faith in Christ.

Jesus promised this indwelling presence to His disciples: "And I will ask the Father, and he will give you another advocate to help you and be with you forever—the Spirit of truth... You know him, for he lives with you and will be in you" (John 14:16–17 NIV).

Paul repeatedly emphasizes this reality: "Don't you know that you yourselves are God's temple and that God's Spirit dwells in your midst?" (1 Corinthians 3:16 NIV). And again: "Do you not know that your bodies are temples of the Holy Spirit, who is in you, whom you have received from God?" (1 Corinthians 6:19 NIV).

This indwelling presence is transformative. It's not just God being present with us (as He is universally), but God being present in us— working from the inside out to make us more like Christ.

This indwelling presence brings several unique benefits:

- **Guidance:** "The Spirit... will guide you into all the truth" (John 16:13 NIV)

- **Empowerment:** "You will receive power when the Holy Spirit comes on you" (Acts 1:8 NIV)

- **Assurance:** "The Spirit himself testifies with our spirit that we are God's children" (Romans 8:16 NIV)

- **Transformation:** "We... are being transformed into his image with ever-increasing glory, which comes from the Lord, who is the Spirit" (2 Corinthians 3:18 NIV)

The indwelling presence of God is what makes Christian spirituality different from just religion. It's not just about following rules or practicing rituals; it's about experiencing the living God from within.

3. God's Manifest Presence

The third level is God's manifest presence—those special moments when God makes His presence known in tangible, experiential ways.

This is what Moses experienced at the burning bush, what the disciples experienced at the Transfiguration, what the early church experienced at Pentecost.

Scripture describes many such moments:

- Jacob declared, "Surely the LORD is in this place, and I was not aware of it" (Genesis 28:16 NIV)

- Moses spoke with God "face to face, as one speaks to a friend" (Exodus 33:11 NIV)

- Isaiah "saw the Lord, high and exalted, seated on a throne" (Isaiah 6:1 NIV)

- The disciples witnessed Jesus "transfigured before them. His face shone like the sun, and his clothes became as white as the light" (Matthew 17:2 NIV)

These manifestations of God's presence aren't inconsistent with His omnipresence; they're special revelations of a presence that was already there. God doesn't become present in these moments—He makes His existing presence known in extraordinary ways.

Throughout church history, believers have testified to similar experiences—moments when God's presence became undeniably real to their senses. Whether through answered prayer, supernatural guidance, overwhelming peace in crisis, or evident power in worship, God continues to make His presence known in ways that go beyond the intellectual to touch the experiential.

These three levels of God's presence—**universal, indwelling, and manifest**—help us understand the paradox of seeking a God who is already everywhere. We're not looking for God to become present; we're positioning ourselves to experience the presence that's already there.

It's like the sun that shines constantly. We don't need to ask the sun to shine; it already is. But we might need to come out from under the shadows to feel its warmth. Similarly, God's presence is constant, but our experience of it can vary greatly depending on our spiritual posture.

> ## God makes His existing presence known in extraordinary ways.

Mary of Bethany: Understanding the Fragrance of Presence

One of the most powerful illustrations of responding to God's presence appears in John 12, where Mary of Bethany anoints Jesus with expensive perfume just days before His crucifixion. This story reveals profound truths about how we can experience and extend God's omnipresence.

The setting is significant—a dinner at Bethany, the hometown of Lazarus whom Jesus had recently raised from the dead. The atmosphere must have been electric with gratitude and anticipation as people gathered to honor Jesus and see the man who had been brought back to life.

John tells us:

> Six days before the Passover, Jesus came to Bethany, where Lazarus lived, whom Jesus had raised from the dead. Here a dinner was given in Jesus' honor. Martha served, while Lazarus was among those reclining at the table with him. Then Mary took about a pint of pure nard, an expensive perfume; she poured it on Jesus' feet and wiped his feet with her hair. And the house was filled with the fragrance of the perfume (John 12:1–3 NIV).

In Mary's act of worship, we find a beautiful picture of how we can respond to God's omnipresence. Let's examine *three dimensions of fragrance* that emerge from this story.

1. The Physical Fragrance

The most obvious aspect of this story is the physical aroma that filled the house. Nard (or spikenard) was an extremely valuable perfume imported from the mountains of India or Nepal. A pint of pure nard would have cost about a year's wages for an average worker—equivalent to tens of thousands of dollars today.

Mary didn't use this perfume sparingly. She poured out the entire flask, creating such a potent aroma that "the house was filled with the fragrance." Everyone present would have been enveloped in the scent—it was impossible to ignore.

This physical fragrance represents our tangible, external acts of worship. When we gather to sing, pray, serve, give, or participate in communion, we're engaging in physical expressions that acknowledge God's presence. These aren't just religious routines; they're responses to the reality that God is present among us.

In the Old Testament, God instructed His people to burn incense regularly in the Tabernacle and Temple (Exodus 30:8). This wasn't because God needed pleasant aromas, but because the physical fragrance symbolized the prayers and worship going up to Him. It created a sensory reminder of divine presence.

Similarly, our external acts of worship create "sensory reminders" that God is present. They help us move from intellectual acknowledgment of God's omnipresence to experiential awareness of His presence with us.

2. The Spiritual Fragrance

Beyond the physical aroma, Mary's act revealed a deeper spiritual fragrance—the aroma of genuine devotion. This wasn't just a ceremonial gesture; it was an expression of profound love, gratitude, and surrender.

Notice what Mary did:

- She used her most valuable possession

- She broke all social conventions by letting down her hair in public

- She humbled herself to wash Jesus's feet

- She didn't hold anything back

This spiritual fragrance—the genuine condition of her heart—was what made her external act meaningful. Without it, the expensive perfume would have been just another religious performance.

Paul captures this principle in 2 Corinthians 2:15: "For we are to God the pleasing aroma of Christ among those who are being saved and those who are perishing" (2 Corinthians 2:15 NIV). Our lives emit a spiritual fragrance, perceivable to God and influential to others.

When Judas criticized Mary's extravagance, suggesting the perfume should have been sold and the money given to the poor, Jesus defended her: "Leave her alone... She did what she could. She poured perfume on my body beforehand to prepare for my burial" (Mark 14:6, 8 NIV).

Jesus recognized that Mary's act wasn't wasteful extravagance but prophetic worship. She discerned something about Jesus's coming sacrifice that even the disciples had missed. Her spiritual insight led to physical expression that created lasting impact.

3. The Lingering Fragrance

The third dimension is the lingering fragrance—how Mary's act of worship continued to affect others long after the moment had passed.

After her anointing, Jesus carried the fragrance of Mary's worship with Him through all the events of Holy Week. As He entered Jerusalem on Palm Sunday, as He taught in the Temple, as He celebrated the Last Supper, as He prayed in Gethsemane, as He endured trials and scourging—the lingering scent of nard would have remained on His skin and clothes.

Even as Roman soldiers drove nails through His hands and feet, they would have breathed in the aroma of Mary's worship. As Jesus hung on the cross, that fragrance mingled with the scent of His blood and sweat.

What an extraordinary thought: Mary's worship literally accompanied Jesus to the cross. The fragrance she created continued long after her physical act was complete.

This lingering dimension reveals how our worship creates effects that extend beyond the moment. When we genuinely encounter God's presence and respond appropriately, the impact continues in ways we may never fully understand in this life.

Jesus affirmed this lingering impact when He said of Mary, "Truly I tell you, wherever the gospel is preached throughout the world, what she has done will also be told, in memory of her" (Mark 14:9 NIV). Two thousand years later, we're still talking about Mary's act of worship—the ultimate lingering fragrance!

These three dimensions of fragrance—**physical, spiritual, and lingering**—show us how to respond to God being everywhere. We engage in tangible expressions that acknowledge His presence. We ensure those external acts flow from genuine heart devotion. And we trust that the effects of our worship extend beyond what we can see or understand.

> Mary's worship literally
> accompanied Jesus to the cross.

Becoming Carriers of God's Presence

Understanding God's omnipresence should transform not just how we think about God but how we live every day. If God is truly present everywhere, then we should live as conscious carriers of His presence wherever we go.

This concept appears throughout Scripture. When God commissioned Moses at the burning bush, Moses asked, "Who am I that I should go to Pharaoh and bring the Israelites out of Egypt?" God's response is telling: "I will be with you" (Exodus 3:11–12 NIV). Moses's adequacy wasn't based on his own abilities but on God's presence with him.

Similarly, when Jesus gave the Great Commission, He concluded with this promise: "And surely I am with you always, to the very end of the age" (Matthew 28:20 NIV). The disciples' ability to fulfill their mission depended entirely on Jesus's ongoing presence with them.

Paul understood this reality when he wrote, "I can do all this through him who gives me strength" (Philippians 4:13 NIV). His confidence wasn't in his own resources but in the present Christ who empowered him.

So what does it mean to live as a carrier of God's presence? Let me suggest *three practical expressions*.

1. Conscious Awareness

The first step in becoming a carrier of God's presence is developing conscious awareness of His presence with you at all times. This isn't about manufacturing feelings or forcing emotional responses; it's about aligning your mind with the reality that God is already present.

Brother Lawrence, a 17th-century monk, described this as "practicing the presence of God." In his classic book by that title, he explained how he learned to maintain awareness of God's presence whether washing dishes in the monastery kitchen or participating in formal worship.

"The time of business," he wrote, "does not with me differ from the time of prayer, and in the noise and clatter of my kitchen... I possess God in as great tranquility as if I were upon my knees at the blessed sacrament."[2]

This conscious awareness transforms mundane activities into sacred moments. It eliminates the artificial division between "spiritual" and "secular" aspects of life. Everything becomes holy when done in conscious communion with the God who is everywhere.

Practically, you can develop this awareness through:

- Beginning each day by acknowledging God's presence

- Creating "trigger moments" throughout your day to refocus on His presence

- Practicing silence and solitude regularly

- Using Scripture phrases as breath prayers

- Seeing interruptions as divine appointments

---

2   Brother Lawrence, *The Practice of the Presence of God*, trans. John J. Delaney (Garden City, NY: Image Books, 1977).

I've found that setting hourly reminders on my phone has been transformative. When they go off, I pause briefly—sometimes just for a few seconds—to acknowledge God's presence and realign my thoughts with His reality. These micro-moments of awareness gradually reshape how I experience each day.

2. Contagious Influence

The second aspect of carrying God's presence is allowing His presence in you to influence others around you. Like Mary's perfume that filled the entire house with fragrance, God's presence in you should affect the atmosphere wherever you go.

Paul describes this influence in 2 Corinthians 2:14–15: "But thanks be to God, who in Christ always leads us in triumphal procession, and through us spreads the fragrance of the knowledge of him everywhere. For we are the aroma of Christ to God among those who are being saved and among those who are perishing" (2 Corinthians 2:14–15 ESV).

Notice the imagery: we're being led in Christ's victory parade, spreading the knowledge of Him "everywhere" like a pervasive fragrance. This isn't something we manufacture; it's something that happens naturally when we're filled with God's presence.

Think about how fragrances work. They don't have to try to spread; they simply do. A person wearing perfume doesn't have to work at making others smell it. Similarly, when you're genuinely experiencing God's presence, you don't have to force its effect on others; it naturally influences the environments you enter.

I've witnessed this phenomenon countless times. When someone walks into a tense meeting carrying the peace of God's presence, the atmosphere changes. When someone enters a conflict situation carrying God's grace, hardened positions begin to soften. When someone steps into a hopeless circumstance carrying God's faith, new possibilities emerge.

This contagious influence doesn't require extroverted personality, eloquent speech, or dramatic actions. It simply requires being so filled with God's presence that it spills over to affect others. As Jesus said, "Out of the abundance of the heart the mouth speaks" (Matthew 12:34 ESV).

3. Compassionate Action

The third expression of carrying God's presence is compassionate action that extends God's presence to others, especially those in need or crisis.

In Isaiah 58, God addresses people who perform religious rituals while ignoring the needs around them. He then describes the fast He has chosen: "Is it not to share your food with the hungry and to provide the poor wanderer with shelter—when you see the naked, to clothe them, and not to turn away from your own flesh and blood?" (Isaiah 58:7 NIV).

The result of such compassion? "Then your light will break forth like the dawn, and your healing will quickly appear; then your righteousness will go before you, and the glory of the LORD will be your rear guard. Then you will call, and the LORD will answer; you will cry for help, and he will say: Here am I" (Isaiah 58:8–9 NIV).

That final phrase—"Here am I"—is significant. It's God making His presence known in response to compassionate action. When we extend ourselves to meet others' needs, we're creating space for God's presence to be experienced.

Jesus exemplified this in His incarnation. John 1:14 tells us, "The Word became flesh and made his dwelling among us." The phrase "made his dwelling" can be translated "tabernacled" or "pitched his tent"—it's the language of God's presence taking up residence with humanity.

Jesus didn't remain distant from human suffering; He entered fully into it. He touched lepers, ate with outcasts, wept at graves, and ultimately took all human sin upon Himself at the cross. Through His compassionate action, God's presence became tangible to people who had felt abandoned or rejected.

As His followers, we continue this ministry of incarnational presence. When we sit with the grieving, serve the poor, visit the imprisoned, welcome the stranger, or stand with the marginalized, we're making God's omnipresence experientially real to those who might otherwise question His existence or care.

> When we extend ourselves to meet others' needs, we're creating space for God's presence to be experienced.

Living in Response to God's Omnipresence

As we conclude our exploration of God's omnipresence, let me offer three practical responses that will help you experience this divine attribute more fully in your daily life.

1. Cultivate Sacred Awareness

First, develop the habit of sacred awareness—recognizing and acknowledging God's presence throughout your day. Don't compartmentalize your spiritual life to certain times or places, but practice seeing all of life as lived before the face of God.

The ancient Celts had a beautiful concept called "thin places"—locations where the boundary between Heaven and earth seemed especially permeable, where God's presence felt particularly accessible.

While certain physical locations may indeed facilitate awareness of God's presence, the reality is that every place is potentially a "thin place" when we approach it with eyes to see and ears to hear.

Cultivating this awareness might include:

- Beginning each day with a simple acknowledgment: "Lord, you are here. I am in your presence."

- Creating physical reminders in your environment—a cross, a Scripture verse, a meaningful symbol—that prompt awareness of God's presence.

- Developing the habit of brief "presence prayers" during transitional moments in your day—when stopping at a red light, before entering a meeting, while waiting in line.

- Ending each day with an reflection prayer, thinking about where you experienced God's presence and where you missed it.

This sacred awareness transforms how you experience every aspect of life—from the dramatic to the mundane. As you recognize God's presence in all circumstances, you discover that there are no ordinary moments.

2. Create Space for Encounter

Second, while God is everywhere by nature, our experience of His presence often deepens in specific contexts we create intentionally. Just as Mary created space for encountering Jesus through her act of worship, we need to create space for encountering God's presence in our busy lives.

Throughout Scripture, we see people creating such spaces:

- Jacob set up a stone pillar at Bethel to mark where he had encountered God (Genesis 28:18)

- Moses removed his sandals at the burning bush, recognizing the holy ground of God's presence (Exodus 3:5)

- David established a tent for the Ark of the Covenant where worship continued day and night (1 Chronicles 16:1)

- Jesus regularly withdrew to solitary places to pray (Luke 5:16)

Creating space for encounter might include:

- Establishing a consistent time and place for personal devotion

- Participating regularly in corporate worship

- Engaging in extended times of prayer, fasting, or retreat

- Setting aside specific times to listen for God's voice without agenda

- Creating physical spaces in your home dedicated to encountering God

These practices don't make God more present—He already is fully present. Rather, they increase your capacity to experience the presence that's already there. They tune your spiritual senses to recognize divine reality.

3. Carry His Presence Intentionally

Finally, move beyond passive awareness to active commission. God being everywhere isn't just a comfort for your benefit; it's a calling for His purposes. Like Isaiah who heard God ask, "Whom shall I send? And who will go for us?" you're invited to respond, "Here am I. Send me!" (Isaiah 6:8 NIV).

Carrying God's presence intentionally means:

- Entering each environment with the conscious intention of bringing God's presence with you

- Asking regularly, "How can I make God's presence known in this situation?"

- Being available for divine appointments and interruptions

- Moving toward needs and brokenness rather than away from them

- Speaking and acting with the awareness that you represent Christ

One practice that has transformed how I approach this calling is what I call "presence prayers" before significant interactions. Before entering a counseling session, a difficult conversation, a leadership meeting, or even family dinner, I pause briefly to pray: "Lord, make your presence known through me in this situation. Let me carry your peace, your wisdom, your love to these people."

This simple prayer shifts my perspective from self-reliance to God-reliance, from performance pressure to peaceful presence. It reminds me that I'm not responsible for manufacturing results, but for faithfully carrying God's presence into each situation.

Never Truly Alone

As we close this exploration of God's omnipresence, I'm reminded of a powerful moment at a youth retreat years ago. A teenage girl approached me after the final session, tears streaming down her face.

"Pastor Jeff," she said, "I've felt haunted in a way by anxiety when I'm alone. I've grown up in church and I've been around worship all my life. In some places, I feel like an intrusion and see dark things. In other places, I feel like people just tolerate me and I see dark things.

At school, I feel invisible even when I am with people. I've learned to just exist with very dark and lonely thoughts."

She paused, wiping her eyes. "But this weekend, for the first time, I understood that I'm never actually alone. God has been with me in every lonely moment—in both houses, at school, in my room at night. He's been there all along. I just didn't know it."

Her testimony captures the life-changing power of truly grasping God's omnipresence. It doesn't necessarily change our circumstances, but it radically transforms how we experience them. The lonely moments don't disappear, but they're no longer defined by abandonment. The challenging situations don't vanish, but they're no longer faced in isolation.

Wherever you are as you read these words—whatever season you're in, whatever challenges you're facing, whatever emotions you're experiencing—remember this unchanging truth: You are not alone. You have never been alone. You will never be alone.

The God who spoke the universe into existence, who sustains every atom by His power, who orchestrates the movement of galaxies and the migration of birds—this God is personally present with you. Not distant. Not distracted. Not disgusted. Present. Fully, completely, lovingly present.

As the writer of Hebrews reminds us, God Himself has promised: "Never will I leave you; never will I forsake you" (Hebrews 13:5 NIV). This isn't just poetic encouragement; it's the concrete reality of His omnipresence.

You can't go where God is not. You can't face what God doesn't see. You can't experience what God doesn't share. In your highest moments and your lowest valleys, in your greatest achievements and your worst failures, in your deepest questions and your strongest convictions—God is there.

And that, perhaps more than any other truth, changes everything.

Personal Reflection and Small Group Guide

Chapter Summary

This chapter explores God's omnipresence—His existence everywhere at all times. We examined three levels of divine presence: His universal presence throughout creation, His indwelling presence in believers through the Holy Spirit, and His manifest presence in special moments of revelation. Through Mary of Bethany's act of anointing Jesus with perfume, we discovered how worship creates physical, spiritual, and lingering fragrances that acknowledge and extend God's presence. As carriers of God's presence, we're called to cultivate conscious awareness, exert contagious influence, and engage in compassionate action that makes His presence tangible to others. By developing sacred awareness, creating space for encounter, and intentionally carrying His presence, we experience the transformative reality that we are never truly alone.

Key Scripture

"Where can I go from your Spirit? Where can I flee from your presence? If I go up to the heavens, you are there; if I make my bed in the depths, you are there." (Psalm 139:7–8 NIV)

Key Thought

"God doesn't become present in special moments—He makes His existing presence known in extraordinary ways."

Personal Reflection

1. Think about a time when you felt especially aware of God's presence. What circumstances, attitudes, or practices helped you recognize His presence in that moment?

2. Which of the three levels of God's presence (universal, indwelling, manifest) do you find most difficult to grasp or experience? What might help you engage more fully with this dimension?

3. Like Mary of Bethany's expensive perfume, what is your most valuable possession—whether material, emotional, or spiritual—that you could offer as worship to acknowledge God's presence?

4. In what environment (home, workplace, relationships) do you find it most challenging to maintain awareness of God's presence? What specific practice might help you remain conscious of His presence in that context?

5. How might your daily routines and interactions change if you consistently viewed yourself as a carrier of God's presence? Identify one relationship or situation where this perspective would make the most significant difference.

6. What "thin places" have you experienced—locations, activities, or circumstances where God's presence seems especially accessible to you? How might you create more of these opportunities in your regular rhythms?

7. Consider Hebrews 13:5: "Never will I leave you; never will I forsake you." How does this promise specifically address a current challenge, fear, or loneliness you're experiencing?

Small Group Discussion

1. Read John 12:1–8 together. What strikes you most about Mary's act of worship? How does her example challenge or inspire your own response to God's presence?

2. Pastor Jeff describes three dimensions of fragrance from Mary's act: physical, spiritual, and lingering. Share examples of how you've experienced or created each type in your own worship and service.

3. Discuss Brother Lawrence's statement: "The time of business does not with me differ from the time of prayer." What prevents us from experiencing this seamless awareness of God's presence throughout our daily activities?

4. How does our church community currently create space for encountering God's presence? What additional practices or environments might help people more deeply experience His presence among us?

5. Share experiences of how someone else's conscious carrying of God's presence impacted you during a difficult time. What specifically did they do or say that made God's presence more tangible?

6. How might understanding God's omnipresence change how we approach evangelism? If God is already present everywhere, what exactly are we doing when we "bring God" to others?

7. Read Acts 17:24–28 together. Paul tells the Athenians that God is not far from any of us, "for in him we live and move and have our being." How might this perspective change our approach to seekers who feel distant from God?

For Group Leaders

Preparation:

This topic touches deeply on our experience of God in daily life. Before leading this discussion, spend time reflecting on your own journey with God's presence. Be prepared to share honestly about both profound encounters and seasons when God's presence felt distant. Your vulnerability will create space for authentic sharing.

Setting the Tone:

Begin by acknowledging that experiences of God's presence can vary widely. Some group members may have dramatic testimonies of encountering God's manifest presence, while others may connect with Him more subtly or intellectually. Affirm that these differences reflect God's diverse ways of relating to unique individuals, not varying degrees of spirituality.

Facilitation Tips:

- For question #1 about Mary of Bethany, consider having people identify what her act cost her—not just financially, but socially and personally. This helps connect worship to sacrifice.

- When discussing question #3 about Brother Lawrence, be careful not to create guilt in those struggling to maintain awareness of God throughout daily life. Frame this as an aspiration, not an expectation.

- For question #5 about experiencing God's presence through others, be prepared for emotional responses if people share about receiving ministry during grief, trauma, or crisis.

- If discussion of question #6 about evangelism reveals misconceptions, gently redirect without making people feel judged for previous approaches.

Application Focus:

End your time by having each person identify one specific environment this week (a challenging relationship, workplace situation, family dynamic) where they want to be more conscious of God's presence. Pair people up to pray specifically for each other about these environments, and encourage them to check in with their prayer partner midweek. This practical focus helps move the concept of omnipresence from theological understanding to lived experience.

7

STRENGTH UNDER CONTROL

The Omnipotence of God

I'M 6'4" TALL and I am not built to sleep on a tiny couch in an ICU room, but in November and December of 2010, I slept on one for 32 nights. Our 15-month-old baby, Cassidy Kate, was fighting for her life—her tiny body ravaged by a vicious strain of E. coli that shut down her kidneys completely. She went through two kinds of dialysis—peritoneal and hemodialysis—as her doctors tried to keep her alive one hour at a time. I watched machines do what her organs no longer could, and I listened for every beep, breath, and whisper, praying that the God I believed in was still near.

One evening, as I sat beside her bed the doctor came in. Her blood pressure was 161/119. This was beyond dangerous. I sensed desperation. I asked the nurses not to let anyone come in the room for an hour. I was going to anoint her with oil and pray. Before I started, the nurse noticed my distress and said, "You know," she said quietly, "the most powerful thing right now is your presence and God's presence through you. She needs your peace, daddy."

She left the room and I gently anointed her and placed my hand over my daughter's tiny body—not picking it up, not handling her, just resting my palm over her with the lightest pressure. I prayed and didn't look up for one hour. After about one hour, I looked up and the monitor showed her blood pressure to be 119/70. I lost it.

I rushed out of the room and called all of the nurses in to come look.

They all acknowledged the miracle. The one nurse said, "The most powerful force for her healing right now is gentle, controlled strength of the Father through you."

That moment transformed my understanding of what real power looks like. It's not always dramatic, forceful, or obvious. Sometimes the most profound power is strength that's carefully calibrated, intentionally restrained, perfectly controlled.

Years later, I realized this experience had given me a glimpse into the omnipotence of God—His all-powerful nature that operates not through brute force or cosmic bullying, but through strength under perfect control.

> Sometimes the most profound power is strength that's carefully calibrated, intentionally restrained, perfectly controlled.

What Is Omnipotence?

The word *omnipotence* comes from two Latin terms: *omni* meaning 'all' and *potens* meaning 'power.' Simply put, God's omnipotence means He has all power and can do anything that's consistent with His nature and character.

Scripture says this over and over:

- "Ah, Sovereign LORD, you have made the heavens and the earth by your great power and outstretched arm. Nothing is too hard for you" (Jeremiah 32:17 NIV).

- "I know that you can do all things; no purpose of yours can be thwarted" (Job 42:2 NIV).

- "Jesus looked at them and said, 'With man this is impossible, but with God all things are possible'" (Matthew 19:26 NIV).

- "For nothing will be impossible with God" (Luke 1:37 ESV).

At first glance, these verses might suggest God can do literally anything we can imagine. But that's not quite what omnipotence means. The Bible also tells us there are things God cannot do:

- **He cannot lie** (Titus 1:2)

- **He cannot deny Himself** (2 Timothy 2:13)

- **He cannot be tempted by evil** (James 1:13)

These aren't limitations on God's power; they're expressions of His character. God can't lie not because He lacks the power to speak falsehood, but because lying would contradict His nature of perfect truth. God's omnipotence operates within the framework of His other attributes—His holiness, love, wisdom, justice, and truth.

Think of it this way: A master pianist can play anything within the range of what a piano can produce. The piano has limitations. It can't sound like a trumpet or a human voice. But within those parameters, the master can create infinite musical expressions. These "limitations" don't diminish the pianist's mastery; they define the context in which that mastery operates.

Similarly, God being all-powerful doesn't mean He can do logically contradictory things like make a square circle or create a rock so heavy He can't lift it. Such logical impossibilities aren't things at all—they're just nonsensical combinations of words. God's inability to perform logical impossibilities no more limits His omnipotence than a piano's inability to taste like chocolate limits the pianist's skill.

What omnipotence does mean is that God possesses all the power necessary to accomplish His purposes. Nothing can stop Him from fulfilling His plans. No force in the universe can successfully oppose His will. No problem is too complex, no situation too far gone, no need too great for His power to address.

The Lion and the Lamb: Two Aspects of Divine Power

In Revelation 5, John records a heavenly vision where the fate of humanity hangs in the balance. A scroll sealed with seven seals represents God's redemptive plan for creation, but no one in Heaven or on earth is worthy to open it. John weeps at this apparent cosmic deadlock.

Then one of the elders tells him, "Do not weep! See, the Lion of the tribe of Judah, the Root of David, has triumphed. He is able to open the scroll and its seven seals" (Revelation 5:5 NIV).

John turns, expecting to see a mighty lion, but instead sees "a Lamb, looking as if it had been slain, standing at the center of the throne" (Revelation 5:6 NIV).

This contrast reveals something profound about God's all-powerful nature. The elder announces a Lion—symbolizing majesty, strength, and dominance. But what appears is a Lamb—symbolizing gentleness, sacrifice, and apparent weakness. Yet this seeming contradiction resolves in Jesus Christ, who embodies both aspects of divine power.

The Lion: Power as Strength

The lion imagery draws from Genesis 49:9, where Jacob blesses his son Judah: "You are a lion's cub, Judah... He crouches like a lion, who dares to rouse him?" This metaphor speaks of authoritative strength, royal power, and sovereign rule.

In Christ, we see this lion-like aspect of omnipotence displayed in various ways:

- His authoritative teaching: "The crowds were amazed at his teaching, because he taught as one who had authority, and not as their teachers of the law" (Matthew 7:28–29 NIV).

- His command over nature: "He got up, rebuked the wind and said to the waves, 'Quiet! Be still!' Then the wind died down and it was completely calm" (Mark 4:39 NIV).

- His power over disease: "Jesus reached out his hand and touched the man. 'I am willing,' he said. 'Be clean!' Immediately the leprosy left him" (Luke 5:13 NIV).

- His authority over demons: "With authority and power he gives orders to impure spirits and they come out!" (Luke 4:36 NIV).

- His victory over death: "I am the Living One; I was dead, and now look, I am alive for ever and ever! And I hold the keys of death and Hades" (Revelation 1:18 NIV).

This lion-like power commands respect and inspires awe. It's the power that formed galaxies and atoms, that parts seas and raises the dead, who will ultimately judge all creation and establish God's eternal Kingdom.

The Lamb: Power as Sacrifice

Yet when John turns to see this mighty Lion, he sees a slain Lamb. This unexpected image reveals the second aspect of divine omnipotence: power expressed through voluntary sacrifice.

The lamb imagery draws from the Passover tradition, where a spotless lamb's blood protected Israel from judgment. It speaks of redemption through sacrifice, victory through apparent defeat, strength made perfect in weakness.

In Christ, we see this lamb-like aspect of omnipotence displayed:

- In His incarnation: "Who, being in very nature God... made himself nothing by taking the very nature of a servant, being made in human likeness" (Philippians 2:6–7 NIV).

- In His servanthood: "For even the Son of Man did not come to be served, but to serve, and to give his life as a ransom for many" (Mark 10:45 NIV).

- In His suffering: "He was oppressed and afflicted, yet he did not open his mouth; he was led like a lamb to the slaughter" (Isaiah 53:7 NIV).

- In His death: "This is my blood of the covenant, which is poured out for many for the forgiveness of sins" (Matthew 26:28 NIV).

This lamb-like power seems like weakness to the world but accomplishes what brute force never could. It's the power that transforms hearts, that forgives sins, that reconciles enemies, that makes all things new from the inside out.

The amazing thing about divine power is that it includes both the Lion and the Lamb. The Lion conquers through strength; the Lamb conquers through sacrifice. In Jesus, both aspects of power find perfect expression.

The Lion roars, "All authority in heaven and on earth has been given to me" (Matthew 28:18 NIV). The Lamb whispers, "Not my will, but yours be done" (Luke 22:42 NIV).

The Lion declares, "I am the resurrection and the life" (John 11:25 NIV). The Lamb submits, "Father, into your hands I commit my spirit" (Luke 23:46 NIV).

Understanding both faces of God's omnipotence helps us navigate the apparent contradictions in our own experiences of divine power. Sometimes God displays lion-like power through dramatic intervention in our circumstances. Other times He displays lamb-like power through sustaining us in suffering we don't understand. Both are expressions of the same power, working for the same redemptive purpose.

> The Lion conquers through strength;
> the Lamb conquers through sacrifice.

Omnipotent Grace: Poised in Power

In the next and final chapter, we'll explore in more depth how these two aspects of God's power—lion-like strength and lamb-like sacrifice—come together in what I call "omnipotent grace." This is the perfect combination of unlimited power and perfect love that defines how God relates to us.

For now, let's focus on how this all-powerful grace was displayed in Christ, particularly in how He was "poised in power"—perfectly balanced between strength and restraint.

The Greek word that best captures this concept is *prautes,* often translated as 'meekness' or 'gentleness.' This term doesn't suggest weakness, as modern English might imply, but rather "strength under control." It describes a powerful horse that has been trained to respond to the slightest touch of the reins—not a reduction of strength, but the disciplined channeling of that strength.

Jesus claimed this quality for Himself when He said, "Take my yoke upon you and learn from me, for I am gentle [*prautes*] and humble in heart, and you will find rest for your souls" (Matthew 11:29 NIV).

This controlled strength manifested in several ways throughout Jesus's ministry:

1. In His Response to Opposition

When Jesus faced opposition, He never reacted from insecurity or defensiveness. He never used His divine power to crush critics or silence doubters. Instead, He responded with perfectly calibrated strength—sometimes with penetrating questions, sometimes with convicting parables, sometimes with strategic silence.

When religious leaders tried to trap Him with the question about paying taxes to Caesar, He didn't destroy them with divine fire or even with scathing rebuke. He simply asked for a coin and said, "Give back to Caesar what is Caesar's, and to God what is God's" (Matthew 22:21 NIV)—an answer so perfectly balanced that it left His opponents speechless.

When standing before Pilate during His trial, Jesus demonstrated the same poise. Pilate declared, "Don't you realize I have power either to free you or to crucify you?" Jesus replied, "You would have no power over me if it were not given to you from above" (John 19:10–11 NIV). Even facing execution, Jesus remained centered in the knowledge of His Father's sovereign power working through apparent powerlessness.

2. In His Miracles and Ministry

Jesus's miracles displayed tremendous power, but always power exercised with precise purpose and perfect control. He never performed miracles as spectacles or to impress crowds. He refused Satan's temptation to jump from the Temple pinnacle, though He certainly could have done so and survived.

Notice how specifically targeted His miracles were—addressing genuine human need rather than demonstrating raw power. He could have leveled mountains or created islands, but instead He healed the sick, fed the hungry, calmed storms threatening His disciples, and raised the dead to comfort grieving families.

Even His most dramatic displays of power, like the feeding of the 5,000, were marked by order and sufficiency rather than extravagance. The miracle produced exactly enough food, with twelve baskets of leftovers—not a hundred or a thousand.

3. In His Management of Time and Energy

Jesus also demonstrated strength under control in how He managed His time and energy. Though surrounded by overwhelming need, He never allowed urgency to override importance. He maintained rhythms of ministry and retreat, engagement and solitude, public teaching, and private prayer.

When the crowds pressed in with their needs, He sometimes withdrew to lonely places to pray (Luke 5:16). Not because He lacked compassion, but because He understood the necessity of aligning His human strength with the Father's purposes.

He knew when to say yes and when to say no. He knew when to heal immediately and when to delay (as with Lazarus). He knew when to speak publicly and when to instruct His disciples to tell no one. This wasn't indecision or inconsistency, but perfect discernment of the Father's timing.

4. In His Path to the Cross

Perhaps the most profound display of Jesus's controlled strength was His journey to the cross. At any point, He could have abandoned the path of suffering. In the Garden of Gethsemane, He reminded Peter,

"Do you think I cannot call on my Father, and he will at once put at my disposal more than twelve legions of angels?" (Matthew 26:53 NIV).

Jesus had the power to obliterate His enemies, escape His captors, or simply vanish from the cross. Instead, He channeled His omnipotence into endurance—the strength to suffer unjustly, to bear unimaginable pain, to carry the weight of the world's sin.

Peter, who witnessed this firsthand, would later write, "When they hurled their insults at him, he did not retaliate; when he suffered, he made no threats. Instead, he entrusted himself to him who judges justly" (1 Peter 2:23 NIV).

This is omnipotence in its most sublime expression—not the absence of power, but the perfect application of power in accordance with love's highest purpose.

Experiencing God's Power in Our Weakness

One of the most paradoxical aspects of God's omnipotence is how it operates through human weakness. This runs contrary to our natural thinking. We typically assume power is most effective when paired with strength, resources, and capability. But God's economy works differently.

Paul discovered this truth through his experience with what he called a "thorn in the flesh"—some unspecified affliction that caused him ongoing distress. After praying three times for God to remove it, he received this response: "My grace is sufficient for you, for my power is made perfect in weakness" (2 Corinthians 12:9 NIV).

This revelation transformed Paul's perspective: "Therefore I will boast all the more gladly about my weaknesses, so that Christ's power may rest on me. That is why, for Christ's sake, I delight in weaknesses, in insults, in hardships, in persecutions, in difficulties. For when I am weak, then I am strong" (2 Corinthians 12:9–10 NIV).

Paul wasn't celebrating weakness for its own sake or adopting a martyr complex. He was recognizing a profound spiritual principle: God's omnipotence operates most visibly and effectively when human strength is removed from the equation.

This pattern appears throughout Scripture:

- God chose Abraham and Sarah to birth a nation when they were far beyond childbearing age.

- God called Moses to confront Pharaoh despite his speech impediment.

- God appointed Gideon to defeat the Midianite army after reducing his forces from 32,000 to just 300 men.

- God selected David, the youngest and least impressive of Jesse's sons, to become Israel's greatest king.

- God established the early church through uneducated fishermen and former tax collectors.

In each case, human inadequacy became the stage on which divine adequacy was displayed. This wasn't coincidental but intentional. As Paul explained, God deliberately "chose the foolish things of the world to shame the wise; God chose the weak things of the world to shame the strong... so that no one may boast before him" (1 Corinthians 1:27, 29 NIV).

I've witnessed this principle countless times in ministry. The most powerful testimonies often come from the most broken lives. The most effective servants are frequently those who recognize their utter dependence on God's strength. The most transformative ministries typically emerge from the deepest needs.

I remember working with a couple who was struggling after two consecutive affairs. In most cases, there is no hope of forgiveness, hope, or healing. We worked through the phases of relational restoration. They each worked very hard to rebuild their marriage.

> The most powerful testimonies often come from the most broken lives.

Against all odds, their marriage not only survived but eventually was restored. Today they are getting back on their feet and slowly starting to discuss ways to make a difference with others. As God continues to work in them and as they continue to strengthen their marriage, their testimony will touch lives powerfully because their story showcases God's power, not their own capability. They're truly just broken people serving a powerful God.

This pattern of strength-in-weakness isn't just about what God does through us; it's about what He does in us. Our weakness becomes the access point for experiencing His power in transformative ways. When we come to the end of our resources, we discover the beginning of His. When our strength fails, His can finally take over.

Mary's Magnificat (song) beautifully expresses this reality: "He has performed mighty deeds with his arm; he has scattered those who are proud in their inmost thoughts. He has brought down rulers from their thrones but has lifted up the humble" (Luke 1:51–52 NIV).

In God's Kingdom, weakness isn't a barrier to experiencing His omnipotence; it's the prerequisite.

Finding Hope in God's Power

God's all-powerful nature isn't just a theological concept; it's a practical source of hope for every circumstance we face. When properly understood, God's omnipotence provides a foundation for responding to life's greatest challenges with confidence and peace.

Let me suggest *three specific ways God's omnipotence offers hope* in our daily lives:

1. Hope in Impossible Situations

We all face situations that seem impossible—relational conflicts that appear irreconcilable, financial problems with no visible solution, health diagnoses with grim prognoses, addictions that have resisted every attempt at recovery.

God's omnipotence means that nothing is impossible with Him. The same power that created the universe from nothing, that parted the Red Sea, that raised Jesus from the dead is available to address your impossible situation.

Abraham understood this when facing the impossibility of having a child in his old age. Romans 4:20–21 tells us, "Yet he did not waver through unbelief regarding the promise of God, but was strengthened in his faith and gave glory to God, being fully persuaded that God had power to do what he had promised" (NIV).

Faith in God's omnipotence doesn't mean denying the reality of the impossible situation. It means believing that what is impossible with man remains possible with God. It means shifting our hope from human solutions to divine intervention.

I've prayed with parents whose children were captive to addiction, with patients facing terminal diagnoses, with couples in seemingly irreconcilable conflict. In each case, faith in God's omnipotence provided not a guarantee of a specific outcome, but the assurance that no situation is beyond the reach of God's redemptive power.

Sometimes God's power works through dramatic intervention—the addiction is suddenly broken, the disease unexpectedly retreats, the relationship miraculously heals. Other times His power works through supernatural endurance—providing strength to face another day, peace that defies explanation, love that persists despite rejection.

Either way, the omnipotence of God means your impossible situation doesn't have the final word.

2. Hope in Personal Inadequacy

Many of us struggle with a deep sense of inadequacy—the feeling that we don't have what it takes to fulfill our responsibilities, overcome our challenges, or become the person God has called us to be.

God's omnipotence means that our inadequacy is never the limiting factor in what He can accomplish in and through us. His power works not despite our weakness but through it.

Moses felt profoundly inadequate when God called him to confront Pharaoh. His objection was direct: "Who am I that I should go to Pharaoh and bring the Israelites out of Egypt?" (Exodus 3:11 NIV). God's response didn't address Moses's inadequacy but promised His adequacy: "I will be with you" (Exodus 3:12 NIV).

The apostle Paul understood this dynamic when he wrote, "I can do all things through him who gives me strength" (Philippians 4:13 NIV). This wasn't positive thinking or self-motivation; it was recognition that God's omnipotence works through surrendered inadequacy.

In my own ministry, I've repeatedly encountered tasks that far exceeded my abilities—counseling situations beyond my expertise, leadership challenges beyond my experience, spiritual warfare beyond my strength. In each case, acknowledging my inadequacy has been the first step toward experiencing God's adequacy.

This doesn't mean we shouldn't develop our skills, expand our knowledge, or strive for excellence. But it does mean that our ultimate confidence rests not in what we bring to the table but in what God provides.

3. Hope in Suffering

Perhaps the greatest test of our belief in God's omnipotence comes in the context of suffering—especially suffering that persists despite our earnest prayers for relief.

If God has all power, why doesn't He use it to eliminate cancer, prevent abuse, stop war, or end poverty? Why does He allow His children to experience pain that He could easily remove?

These questions have no simple answers, but the dual nature of God's power—the Lion and the Lamb—provides a framework for understanding. Sometimes God displays lion-like power by changing our circumstances; other times He shows lamb-like power by changing us within unchanged circumstances.

When Jesus prayed in Gethsemane, "Father, if you are willing, take this cup from me" (Luke 22:42 NIV), He was asking for lion-like intervention—the changing of His circumstances. When He continued, "Yet not my will, but yours be done" (Luke 22:42 NIV), He was submitting to lamb-like transformation—the strength to fulfill His purpose through suffering rather than avoiding it.

God's all-powerful nature gives us hope in suffering not by guaranteeing its removal but by ensuring its redemption. Romans 8:28 assures us that "in all things God works for the good of those who love him, who have been called according to his purpose" (NIV).

This doesn't mean all suffering is good or that God causes every painful circumstance. It means that no suffering is beyond God's redemptive power. What seems like pointless pain in the moment can become the foundation for profound purpose when placed in God's omnipotent hands.

I've witnessed this reality in the lives of countless believers. The woman whose childhood abuse became the catalyst for a ministry to wounded children. The man whose business failure led to the discovery of his true calling. The parents whose child's death sparked a movement that has saved thousands of lives.

None of these people would have chosen their suffering. All of them would have preferred lion-like deliverance from their circumstances. Yet through their pain, they experienced lamb-like transformation that revealed God's power in unexpected ways.

As Paul discovered, sometimes God's answer to our prayers for deliverance is not "I will remove this" but "My grace is sufficient for you, for my power is made perfect in weakness" (2 Corinthians 12:9 NIV).

Strength Under His Control

As we conclude our exploration of God's omnipotence, I want to focus on a practical question: How do we live in proper relationship to the all-powerful God?

Some Christians live in virtual denial of God's omnipotence. They pray timid prayers, expect minimal intervention, and effectively operate as functional atheists most of the time. Others swing to the opposite extreme, treating God's power as a force they can manipulate through the right techniques, formulas, or spiritual gymnastics.

A biblical approach to God's omnipotence involves neither denial nor manipulation, but surrender—placing ourselves under the control of His perfect strength.

Jesus modeled this surrender in His prayer at Gethsemane: "Not my will, but yours be done" (Luke 22:42 NIV). This wasn't passive resignation but active alignment with the Father's purposes. It wasn't abandoning desire but subordinating desire to a higher wisdom and power.

When we pray "your kingdom come, your will be done, on earth as it is in heaven" (Matthew 6:10 NIV), we're expressing the same surrender. We're acknowledging that God's power is always at work according to His purposes, and we're aligning ourselves with those purposes rather than demanding that His power serve our agendas.

Practically, living under God's strength means:

1. Praying Bold Prayers with Humble Hearts

God's omnipotence encourages bold, faith-filled prayer. Jesus taught us to ask, seek, and knock with confidence that our Father wants to give good gifts to His children (Matthew 7:7–11). The same power that raised Christ from the dead is available to address our needs.

Yet this boldness must be balanced with humility. We pray confidently not because we've figured out how to manipulate God's power, but because we trust His character. We recognize that His wisdom may lead to different answers than we expect, and His timing may not match our preferences.

James captures this balance when he writes, "You do not have because you do not ask God. When you ask, you do not receive, because you ask with wrong motives, that you may spend what you get on your pleasures" (James 4:2–3 NIV). Bold asking combined with pure motives positions us to experience God's power appropriately.

2. Working Diligently While Depending Completely

God's all-powerful nature doesn't eliminate our responsibility to act. Throughout Scripture, God's power works through human obedience and effort, not apart from it. Moses had to stretch out his staff over the Red Sea. Joshua had to march around Jericho. The disciples had to distribute the loaves and fish. The early church had to go and preach the gospel.

Yet this human activity must be undergirded by complete dependence on God's power. As Paul writes, "Work out your salvation with fear and trembling, for it is God who works in you to will and to act in order to fulfill his good purpose" (Philippians 2:12–13 NIV).

This paradoxical combination of human effort and divine empowerment characterizes healthy engagement with God's omnipotence. We work as if everything depends on us while trusting as if everything depends on God—because in different senses, both are true.

3. Accepting Mystery While Affirming Truth

Finally, living under God's strength means holding the tension between what we know and what we don't know about His power. We affirm the clear biblical truths: God is all-powerful, God is all-loving, God is actively working for our good and His glory. Yet we also acknowledge the mysteries: Why God's power works dramatically in some situations but not others, why some prayers receive immediate answers while others seem to go unanswered, why suffering persists even for the most faithful believers.

Job's story illustrates this tension. After questioning God's ways and receiving God's response from the whirlwind, Job declares, "Surely I spoke of things I did not understand, things too wonderful for me to know... My ears had heard of you but now my eyes have seen you" (Job 42:3, 5 NIV).

Job doesn't receive explanations for his suffering, but he receives something better—a direct encounter with the omnipotent God. This encounter doesn't eliminate the mystery, but it provides a foundation for trust despite the mystery.

> Job doesn't receive explanations for his suffering, but he receives something better— a direct encounter with the omnipotent God.

The Ultimate Display of God's All-Powerful Grace

As we bring our exploration of God's omnipotence to a close, I'm struck by the perfect integration of power and love displayed at the cross. Here we see omnipotent grace in its ultimate expression—the Lion becoming the Lamb for our salvation.

The cross reveals the seeming paradox of God's power. The Creator of the universe allows Himself to be nailed to wooden beams. The one who commanded the elements submits to brutal execution. The Lord of life experiences death.

To human eyes, the cross looks like weakness, defeat, failure. Yet in this apparent powerlessness, God was displaying His most profound power—the power to redeem sin, defeat death, and reconcile humanity to Himself.

As Paul writes, "For the message of the cross is foolishness to those who are perishing, but to us who are being saved it is the power of God" (1 Corinthians 1:18 NIV). And again, "He was crucified in weakness, yet he lives by God's power" (2 Corinthians 13:4 NIV).

At the cross, we see both faces of divine power:

- **The Lion's power** to bear the weight of the world's sin, to conquer death from the inside, to accomplish what no human power could achieve.

- **The Lamb's power** to surrender willingly, to love sacrificially, to transform through suffering rather than avoiding it.

When Jesus cried, "It is finished" (John 19:30 NIV), He wasn't declaring defeat but victory. The redemption work was complete. The purpose of incarnation was fulfilled. The plan established before the foundation of the world was accomplished.

And three days later, when the stone was rolled away from the empty tomb, the full extent of God's omnipotence was revealed. Death could not hold Him. The grave could not contain Him. Sin's power was broken. Satan's defeat was secured.

This is the all-powerful grace that saves us—not just the raw power to create universes, but the targeted power to recreate human hearts. Not just the capacity to control external circumstances, but the ability to transform internal realities. Not just strength displayed in might, but strength revealed in mercy.

As you face your own challenges, limitations, weaknesses, and impossibilities, remember the Lion and the Lamb. Remember that God's power operates both through changing your circumstances and through changing you within unchanged circumstances. Remember that what looks like weakness may actually be strength under perfect control.

And remember the nurse's words that helped me understand God's power in the NICU: "The most powerful force right now is gentle, controlled strength."

Personal Reflection and Small Group Guide

Chapter Summary

This chapter explores God's omnipotence—His all-powerful nature that can accomplish anything consistent with His character. Through the imagery of the Lion and the Lamb in Revelation 5, we discover two complementary aspects of divine power: lion-like strength that creates and commands, and lamb-like sacrifice that redeems and transforms. Jesus demonstrated "strength under control" throughout His ministry—responding to opposition with poise, performing miracles with purpose, managing time with wisdom, and enduring the cross with resolve. God's power operates most visibly through human weakness, offering hope amid impossible situations, personal inadequacy, and persistent suffering. The cross reveals omnipotence in its most profound expression—not as brute force but as sacrificial love that conquers sin and death through apparent weakness.

Key Scripture

"I know that you can do all things; no purpose of yours can be thwarted." (Job 42:2 NIV)

Key Thought

"Sometimes the most profound power is strength that's carefully calibrated, intentionally restrained, perfectly controlled."

Personal Reflection

1. When have you experienced God's power working through your weakness rather than your strength? What did this teach you about how divine omnipotence operates?

2. Which aspect of God's power do you find yourself more naturally drawn to—the lion-like strength or the lamb-like sacrifice? How might developing a fuller appreciation of the other aspect enrich your relationship with God?

3. Consider a current "impossible" situation in your life. How does God's omnipotence specifically address this circumstance? What would genuine trust in His power look like in this situation?

4. Jesus described Himself as "meek" (*prautes*)—displaying strength under control. In what areas of your life do you need to develop this same quality of controlled strength?

5. Paul wrote, "When I am weak, then I am strong" (2 Corinthians 12:10). What weakness or limitation are you currently resisting that might actually become an access point for experiencing God's power?

6. How has your understanding of unanswered prayer been affected by this chapter's discussion of God's lion-like and lamb-like power? What prayer situation might need to be reframed in light of this understanding?

7. The cross demonstrated that apparent weakness can be the vehicle for God's greatest power. Where in your life might God be working powerfully through what appears to be weakness, failure, or loss?

Small Group Discussion

1. Read Revelation 5:1–14 together. What strikes you about how divine power is portrayed in this passage? How does the contrast between the announced Lion and the appearing Lamb reshape your understanding of God's omnipotence?

2. Pastor Jeff states, "Understanding both faces of God's omnipotence helps us navigate the apparent paradoxes in our own experiences of divine power." Share experiences where you've witnessed both lion-like intervention and lamb-like transformation in your life or the lives of others.

3. Discuss Jesus's statement, "My grace is sufficient for you, for my power is made perfect in weakness" (2 Corinthians 12:9). Why do you think God chooses to display His power primarily through human weakness rather than strength?

4. How might our church community better reflect both aspects of God's power—the strength of the Lion and the sacrifice of the Lamb? In what areas might we be emphasizing one at the expense of the other?

5. Pastor Jeff writes, "Acknowledging our inadequacy is the first step toward experiencing God's adequacy." Share about a time when admitting your limitations opened the door to experiencing God's sufficiency in a new way.

6. Discuss how understanding God's omnipotence as "strength under control" might change our approach to areas like parenting, leadership, conflict resolution, or evangelism.

7. Read 1 Corinthians 1:18–31 together. How does the cross challenge worldly understandings of power and weakness? What implications does this have for how we view success, influence, and effectiveness in Christian life and ministry?

For Group Leaders

Preparation:

This topic touches on profound theological questions about God's power in relation to human suffering and apparent divine inaction. Before leading this discussion, prepare your own heart by reflecting on how you've experienced both aspects of God's power—dramatic intervention and sustaining grace through unchanged circumstances. Be ready to share vulnerably about times when you've wrestled with questions about God's power in your own life.

Setting the Tone:

Begin by acknowledging that many people come to this topic with pain, confusion, or disappointment related to prayers that seemed unanswered or situations where God's power didn't manifest as expected. Create a safe environment where people can express honest questions without receiving simplistic answers or spiritual platitudes.

Facilitation Tips:

- For question #1 about Revelation 5, consider having the passage read aloud twice—once focusing on what is heard (the Lion) and once on what is seen (the Lamb). This helps emphasize the contrast.

- When discussing question #3 about power in weakness, be sensitive to those currently experiencing difficult circumstances. The goal is not to glorify suffering but to find hope within it.

- For question #4 about church community, guide the conversation toward specific, constructive applications rather than general critique. How might your group be a place where both aspects of God's power are honored?

- For question #7 about worldly power versus the cross creates tension, acknowledge that we all absorb cultural definitions of success and power. This is an ongoing area of transformation for every believer.

Application Focus:

End your time by having each person identify one specific situation this week where they need to trust in God's omnipotence. This might be an "impossible" circumstance requiring lion-like intervention, a persistent difficulty requiring lamb-like endurance, or a relationship needing the calibrated strength of "meekness." Have group members pair up to pray specifically for each other about these situations, and encourage them to check in with their prayer partner midweek to share how God's power is manifesting in expected or unexpected ways.

8

BEYOND THE CLASSROOM

Putting God's Attributes into Practice

I STILL REMEMBER the very first Sunday I was scheduled to preach at the Elkton Road Church in Greenville, KY. It was just a Sunday night message. They were considering hiring me but it was so much more than that for me.

I spent hours preparing. I wrote out every word. Multiple times. I practiced in front of a mirror up until it was time to go up to the church building. I memorized Scripture references and crafted what I thought were perfect illustrations.

When the moment came, I walked to the front, legs shaking nervously, heart pounding in my chest. I stood up to preach and I couldn't remember anything I had prepared. I had notes to read, but I wanted to preach it from the heart, not the paper.

After what felt like an eternity (but was probably ten seconds), I said, "Let's pray." That simple statement broke the awkwardness. I nodded, closed my eyes, and somehow found my voice in prayer. I remember a statement that I repeated every time I shared the gospel with someone from my youth until that moment. I'd always pray the same thing as we started a Bible study. That phrase was real inside me. It came out without even planning it.

"Father, I know you're here tonight. You love these people more than I do. They came to hear from you and not a man; so, I ask you to speak. In Jesus' name, amen."

Something shifted in that moment. I opened my eyes and began to speak, not from my carefully crafted notes, but from the overflow of what God had been teaching me. I still stumbled and rambled a bit, but there was a freedom and authenticity that hadn't been there before. I have preached thousands of times since then and every sermon I ever preach always has that same prayer somewhere in the first few minutes. It's a truth in my core.

We all want the real thing. We want to hear God, not just human thinking and talking. He's bigger than we think.

The principle of that prayer has guided my approach to faith for decades since. Theology isn't just for knowing; it's for living. Understanding God's attributes—His holiness, immutability, sovereignty, personal presence, omniscience, omnipresence, and omnipotence—isn't merely an intellectual exercise. It's meant to transform how we navigate every aspect of daily life. We're all here to hear from and know God, the real thing.

> ## Theology isn't just for knowing; it's for living.

From Understanding to Application

Throughout this book, we've explored seven attributes of God that reveal His character and nature. We've seen Him as:

- **Holy**—utterly unique and set apart from all creation

- **Immutable**—unchanging in His nature, character, and promises

- **Sovereign**—ruling supremely over the universe and every human heart

- **Personal**—engaging with us individually while respecting our freedom

- **Omniscient**—knowing everything about us completely and perfectly

- **Omnipresent**—existing everywhere simultaneously and fully

- **Omnipotent**—possessing all power yet applying it with perfect control

Each of these attributes reveals something essential about who God is. But knowledge without application leads to spiritual stagnation. As James warns, "Do not merely listen to the word, and so deceive yourselves. Do what it says" (James 1:22 NIV).

So how do we move from theological understanding to practical application? How do we translate these divine attributes into daily disciplines, decisions, and directions?

The key is living in response rather than reaction. Reaction is instinctive, automatic, and often driven by our limited perspectives and fallen nature. Response is intentional, thoughtful, and shaped by what we know to be true about God.

This is important: From this point forward in this chapter, I'll use more everyday language to talk about God's attributes. Instead of saying omniscience, I'll say all-knowing nature. Instead of omnipresence, I'll say being everywhere. Instead of omnipotence, I'll say all-powerful nature. Instead of immutability, I'll say unchanging nature. I'm making this shift in this chapter because church words can sometimes create distance between us and the reality they describe. But God's character isn't distant or academic—it's personal and life-changing. So let's talk about it in ways that make it real and accessible."

Let me suggest *eight practical ways to live in response* to what you've learned about God's attributes. These aren't quick fixes or simple formulas, but ongoing practices that gradually align our lives with divine reality.

1. Develop Daily Awareness Practices

The gap between knowing truth about God and living it often comes down to simple awareness. We forget what we know. We get caught up in the immediate and lose sight of the eternal. We focus on what's visible and neglect what's real.

Developing daily awareness practices helps bridge this gap. These are intentional habits that remind us of who God is and who we are in relationship to Him. They don't have to be complicated or time-consuming; they just need to be consistent.

Here are *five practical awareness practices* you might consider:

1. **Morning Alignment**—Begin each day by acknowledging God's presence and aligning yourself with His purposes. This can be as simple as declaring, "Lord, you are holy, unchanging, sovereign, personal, all-knowing, ever-present, and all-powerful. I align myself with your character and purposes today." I always start my day with at least one hour alone with the Lord. I almost never miss. I structure my sleep around being able to get up early enough to have time with Him.

2. **Attribute Focus**—Choose one divine attribute to focus on each day or week. Set reminders on your phone, place sticky notes in strategic locations, or use transitions in your day (like stopping at red lights or waiting in lines) to reflect on how this attribute applies to your current circumstances.

3. **Breath Prayers**—Link short prayers to your breathing rhythm as a way to stay connected to God throughout the day. For example:

- Inhale: "You are holy..." / Exhale: "...make me holy."

- Inhale: "You never change..." / Exhale: "...be my rock today."

- Inhale: "You are sovereign..." / Exhale: "...I trust your plan."

4. Creation Triggers—Use regular encounters with creation to remind you of God's attributes. The stability of mountains can remind you of His unchanging nature. The intricacy of a flower can speak of His all-knowing nature. The vastness of the night sky can declare His sovereignty.

5. Gratitude Practice—End each day by identifying and thanking God for specific ways you experienced His attributes. This isn't just general gratitude but specifically connecting your experiences to what you know about His character.

If you are a young mother, you can implement awareness practices in your hectic life with the kids you're raising. Place attribute-themed sticky notes around your house—"God is present" on the bathroom mirror, "God is unchanging" on the refrigerator, "God is all-powerful" above the diaper changing table. These simple reminders will transform mundane moments into sacred encounters.

You could be elbow deep in diaper changing, look up and see 'God is all-powerful,' and suddenly remember that the God who created the universe is with you in that unglamorous moment. It will change everything about how you experience motherhood.

2. Align Your Identity with Divine Truth

Many of our struggles stem from identity confusion—not knowing or forgetting who we really are. We try to construct our identity around changeable factors like our achievements, relationships, appearance, possessions, or social status. When these inevitably shift, our sense of self becomes unstable.

God's attributes provide an unchanging foundation for healthy identity. Understanding who God is clarifies who we are in relationship to Him.

Here's how specific divine attributes shape our identity:

- **God's Holiness** → I am set apart for unique purpose, called to reflect His character.

- **God's Unchanging Nature** → My value doesn't fluctuate with circumstances or performance.

- **God's Sovereignty** → My life has meaning within His larger purposes.

- **God's Personal Nature** → I am known, loved, and engaged with individually.

- **God's All-Knowing Nature** → I'm fully known yet fully loved; nothing about me surprises God.

- **God's Being Everywhere** → I'm never alone, even in my darkest or most isolated moments.

- **God's All-Powerful Nature** → I can face impossible situations through His strength, not mine.

> ## Understanding who God is clarifies who we are in relationship to Him.

To align your identity with these truths, start by identifying false sources of identity. Ask yourself: "Where am I looking for value, worth, or significance apart from who I am in Christ?" Common false identity sources include work (what I accomplish), relationships (who accepts me), appearance (how I look), possessions (what I own), or reputation (what others think of me).

Then, create identity declarations based on God's attributes. These aren't just positive affirmations but statements of truth about who God is and who you are in light of His nature. For example:

- "Because God is holy, I am set apart for His purposes, not defined by worldly standards."

- "Because God is unchanging, my value doesn't fluctuate with my performance."

- "Because God knows everything about me and still loves me, I don't need to pretend or perform."

Repeat these declarations regularly—especially in moments when false identities threaten to reclaim territory in your heart.

I witnessed the power of identity realignment in a man who had built his entire sense of self around his successful career. When an economic downturn led to him losing his job, his identity crumbled. During that season, he began to internalize the truth that his value came from being known and loved by the unchanging God, not from his professional achievements.

"I had to remind myself daily, sometimes hourly, who I really was," he told me. "Not a job title, not a salary figure, but a child of God, known by Him before I was born, loved unconditionally, and part of His eternal purposes."

By the time he found new employment, his identity had shifted. He still worked diligently and pursued excellence, but his sense of self no longer rose and fell with professional success or failure. He had found a more stable foundation in who God is.

3. Transform Decision-Making Processes

Every day, we make countless decisions—from the trivial (what to eat for breakfast) to the momentous (who to marry, what career to pursue, where to live). Most of us have developed decision-making patterns that operate largely on autopilot, based on convenience, comfort, cultural norms, or personal preference.

Understanding God's attributes provides a different framework for decision-making. Instead of just asking, "What do I want?" or "What's easiest?" we can ask, "What aligns with who God is and who He's calling me to be?"

Try implementing this decision-making matrix based on God's attributes:

- **Holiness Filter:** Does this choice set me apart for God's purposes or conform me to the world's patterns?

- **Unchanging Nature Check:** Am I basing this decision on changeable factors or eternal principles?

- **Sovereignty Perspective:** How does this decision fit within God's larger purposes, not just my immediate desires?

- **Personal Connection:** Have I consulted God personally about this, or am I relying solely on my own thinking?

- **All-Knowing Recognition:** Am I acknowledging that God sees factors I can't see, or am I acting as if my limited perspective is complete?

- **Everywhere Awareness:** How does this decision affect my experience of God's presence? Will it enhance or hinder my awareness of Him?

- **All-Powerful Access:** Am I facing this decision in my own strength or accessing God's power through dependence and obedience?

This process doesn't provide easy formulas—it often raises more questions than it answers initially. But it gradually reshapes how we approach choices, aligning our decisions with divine reality rather than temporary concerns.

I've used this framework with couples making major life decisions like job relocations, house purchases, or having children. One couple was torn about whether to accept a lucrative job offer that would require moving away from their supportive church community. On paper, the job looked perfect—better pay, better benefits, better title. But when they applied the decision-making matrix, they realized they were focusing primarily on changeable factors rather than eternal principles.

The sovereignty perspective particularly impacted them. "We started asking how this move would affect our participation in God's larger purposes," the husband told me. "The new job would advance my career but potentially diminish our ministry involvement. We realized we were making decisions based on American dream values rather than Kingdom values."

They ultimately declined the offer, choosing to prioritize their spiritual community and ministry opportunities over career advancement. Three years later, the husband was offered an even better position locally—one that allowed them to maintain their spiritual connections while still advancing professionally.

"Looking back," he reflected, "we can see God's wisdom in having us wait. But at the time, it felt like we were giving up a sure thing for an uncertainty. Understanding God's attributes gave us confidence to make that countercultural choice."

4. Reshape Prayer Patterns

Prayer is our primary means of communication with God, yet many of us fall into repetitive patterns that focus more on our desires than on God's character. Understanding divine attributes transforms how we pray—not just what we ask for, but how we approach the conversation.

Consider how each attribute might reshape your prayer life:

- **Holiness:** Instead of praying primarily for comfort or ease, pray for purification and alignment with God's set-apart purposes. Ask not just for solutions to problems but for sanctification through them.

- **Unchanging Nature:** Ground your prayers in God's unchanging promises rather than fluctuating feelings. Begin prayer by declaring what you know to be eternally true about God, even when current circumstances seem to contradict it.

- **Sovereignty:** Pray with confidence that God is working all things together for good, even when the immediate situation appears chaotic. Use phrases like "I trust that you are sovereign over this situation, even though I don't understand it."

- **Personal Sovereignty:** Balance bold asking with humble submission. Express your desires honestly while surrendering to God's wisdom about whether, when, and how to answer.

- **All-Knowing Nature:** Instead of explaining every detail to God as if He doesn't already know, focus on aligning your perspective with His. Ask questions like, "How do you see this situation?" or "What am I missing here?"

- **Being Everywhere:** Acknowledge God's presence in all circumstances, not just in obviously "spiritual" contexts. Pray about everyday activities, recognizing that no aspect of life is outside His presence or concern.

- **All-Powerful Nature:** Pray with bold faith for impossible situations while recognizing that God's power sometimes works through transformation rather than elimination of challenges. Express both confidence in His ability and trust in His methods.

One practical way to implement this approach is through attribute-based prayer cycles. Rather than always praying in the same pattern, focus on a different divine attribute each day of the week, allowing that aspect of God's nature to shape your prayers.

> Understanding divine attributes transforms how we pray—not just what we ask for, but how we approach the conversation.

For example:

- **Monday: Holiness prayers** (focus on purification and set-apart purpose)

- **Tuesday: Unchanging nature prayers** (focus on God's unchanging promises and character)

- **Wednesday: Sovereignty prayers** (focus on God's overarching purposes)

- **Thursday: Personal prayers** (focus on intimate relationship and communion)

- **Friday: All-knowing prayers** (focus on God's perfect knowledge and perspective)

- **Saturday: Everywhere prayers** (focus on awareness of God in all contexts)

- **Sunday: All-powerful prayers** (focus on God's power working in and through all situations)

A woman in our church shared how this approach revolutionized her prayer life after twenty years of following the same prayer formula. "I used to pray almost exclusively for God to fix problems," she said. "Now I pray for Him to reveal more of His character through those problems. I've gone from treating God like a cosmic vending machine to experiencing Him as a loving Father who's forming me through all circumstances."

5. Reframe Suffering and Challenges

Perhaps the most difficult application of God's attributes comes in how we understand and respond to suffering. When facing illness, loss, betrayal, financial hardship, or any other painful circumstance, our natural tendency is to question God's character or presence.

Understanding God's attributes provides a framework for reframing suffering—not eliminating the pain, but finding meaning and hope within it.

Consider these perspective shifts:

- **From "God isn't holy" to "God is using this to make me holy."** When suffering strikes, we often assume God has failed to maintain the moral order. A holiness perspective recognizes that God may be using painful circumstances to set us apart more completely for His purposes, burning away what's impure and strengthening what's eternal.

- **From "God has changed" to "My circumstances have changed, but God hasn't."** Suffering can make us feel that God has altered His disposition toward us—that He once was for us but now is against us. An immutability perspective anchors us in the unchanging love and faithfulness of God, even when everything else seems unstable.

- **From "God has lost control" to "God is working at a level I can't yet see."** When chaos erupts in our lives, we may wonder if God has somehow lost His grip on the situation. A sovereignty perspective reminds us that God is orchestrating events according to purposes more comprehensive than our immediate comfort.

- **From "God doesn't care about me" to "God is personally engaged with me through this difficulty."** Suffering often feels impersonal—like we're being crushed by blind forces or random events. A personal sovereignty perspective helps us recognize God's intimate involvement, allowing painful circumstances while actively working through them.

- **From "God doesn't understand" to "God knows exactly what I'm going through."** When in pain, we sometimes think no one, not even God, truly understands the depth of our suffering. An all-knowing perspective reminds us that God comprehends our experience more completely than we do ourselves.

- **From "God has abandoned me" to "God is more present in this pain than I can perceive."** Suffering can create a sense of divine absence—that God has left us alone in our darkest hour. A being everywhere perspective affirms that God hasn't moved away; our awareness of His presence may have dimmed, but His reality remains.

- **From "God can't help me" to "God's power is being displayed in ways I hadn't anticipated."** When prayers for deliverance go seemingly unanswered, we may question God's power. An all-powerful perspective recognizes that God's strength is sometimes displayed not through changing our circumstances but through sustaining us within them.

I've witnessed this reframing process in countless lives, but perhaps most powerfully in a young couple who lost their child to a rare genetic disorder. In the aftermath of their devastating loss, they didn't deny their pain or pretend to understand God's purposes. But they consistently reframed their suffering through the lens of God's attributes.

"We don't know why God allowed this," the father told me, "but we know who God is. He is holy, so we trust His purposes even when we don't understand them. He is unchanging, so we know His love for us and for our son hasn't diminished. He is sovereign, so nothing about this took Him by surprise. He knows our grief intimately. He is present with us in every moment of pain. And His power is holding us together when we have no strength of our own."

Their faith wasn't simplistic or superficial. They asked hard questions and experienced deep grief. But by continually reorienting themselves to who God is, they found a pathway through their pain that neither denied the reality of suffering nor the reality of God's character.

6. Revitalize Spiritual Disciplines

Spiritual disciplines—practices like Bible study, prayer, fasting, worship, service, and solitude—have been part of Christian tradition for centuries. Yet many believers approach these disciplines either as religious obligations to fulfill or techniques to master.

Understanding God's attributes revitalizes these practices by connecting them to divine reality rather than religious routine. Each discipline becomes a means of engaging with specific aspects of God's nature.

Consider how divine attributes might reshape these common spiritual disciplines:

BIBLE STUDY:

- **Holy God**: Approach Scripture as set-apart revelation, not just another book to analyze.

- **Unchanging God**: Look for consistency in God's character across different biblical contexts.

- **Sovereign God**: Notice how God works His purposes through flawed people and chaotic circumstances.

- **Personal God**: Read not just for information but for relationship, asking, "What is God saying to me here?"

- **All-Knowing God**: Approach the text with humility, recognizing that God sees connections we might miss.

- **Everywhere God**: Study Scripture with awareness that God is present in the reading process itself.

- **All-Powerful God**: Expect transformation through engagement with the living Word.

PRAYER:

- **Holy God**: Include confession and purification, not just requests.

- **Unchanging God**: Pray God's unchanging promises back to Him.

- **Sovereign God**: Align your requests with God's broader purposes.

- **Personal God**: Converse naturally rather than using formulaic language.

- **All-Knowing God**: Spend more time listening and less time informing God of things He already knows.

- **Everywhere God**: Practice continual prayer throughout the day, not just designated prayer times.

- **All-Powerful God**: Pray boldly for impossible situations while trusting God's methods and timing.

WORSHIP:

- **Holy God**: Focus on God's uniqueness and transcendence, not just emotional experience.

- **Unchanging God**: Worship in all circumstances, recognizing that God is worthy regardless of how you feel.

- **Sovereign God**: Acknowledge His rule over every aspect of your life, surrendering control.

- **Personal God**: Express genuine emotion rather than performing for others.

- **All-Knowing God**: Bring your whole self—doubts, fears, joys, hopes—knowing God already sees them.

- **Everywhere God**: Extend worship beyond church gatherings into everyday activities.

- **All-Powerful God**: Expect God to work powerfully in and through your worship.

A man in our church who had practiced spiritual disciplines faithfully for decades shared how this attribute-based approach renewed his spiritual life. "I was going through the motions," he admitted. "Reading my Bible, praying, going to church—but it had become routine. When I started connecting these practices to specific attributes of God, everything changed. I wasn't just doing religious activities; I was engaging with different facets of God's character. It was like going from a black-and-white faith to full color."

The difference wasn't in what he was doing but in why and how he was doing it. By connecting spiritual disciplines to divine attributes, he transformed obligation into relationship—from "I should" to "I get to."

> By connecting spiritual disciplines to divine attributes, he transformed obligation into relationship—from "I should" to "I get to."

7. Renovate Relationship Patterns

Our understanding of God profoundly shapes how we relate to others. If we view God primarily as a harsh judge, we tend to approach relationships with criticism and conditional acceptance. If we see God primarily as an indulgent grandfather, we may lack appropriate boundaries or accountability in relationships.

A balanced understanding of God's attributes helps us renovate relationship patterns to reflect His character more accurately.

Here's how specific attributes might reshape key relationships:

MARRIAGE:

- **Holy God**: View marriage as a sacred covenant, not just a social contract.

- **Unchanging God**: Base commitment on promises and covenant, not just feelings or circumstances.

- **Sovereign God**: Recognize God's purposes for marriage beyond personal happiness.

- **Personal God**: Engage with your spouse as a unique individual, not just a role-filler.

- **All-Knowing God**: Practice vulnerability and honesty, knowing nothing is hidden from God anyway.

- **Everwhere God**: Acknowledge God as an active third party in the marriage relationship.

- **All-Powerful God**: Rely on God's strength rather than your own to sustain commitment through challenges.

PARENTING:

- **Holy God**: Focus on character formation, not just behavior management.

- **Unchanging God**: Provide consistent presence and unconditional love amid changing stages and phases.

- **Sovereign God**: Trust God's overarching purposes for your children beyond your parental plans.

- **Personal God**: Recognize and respect each child's unique design and calling.

- **All-Knowing God**: Listen more than you lecture, seeking to understand your child's perspective.

- **Everywhere God**: Model awareness of God's presence in everyday activities, not just "religious" moments.

- **All-Powerful God**: Release control, recognizing that God's power, not your perfect parenting, ultimately shapes your children.

FRIENDSHIP:

- **Holy God**: Encourage friends toward their highest calling rather than just their comfort.

- **Unchanging God**: Provide stable presence through others' changing circumstances and seasons.

- **Sovereign God**: Recognize divine orchestration in friendships—that God brings people together for purposes beyond enjoyment.

- **Personal God**: Engage with genuine interest in others' unique stories and experiences.

- **All-Knowing God**: Listen with the awareness that you don't see the whole picture of others' lives.

- **Everywhere God**: Acknowledge God's presence in casual interactions, not just in explicitly spiritual conversations.

- **All-Powerful God**: Believe that God can work through your imperfect efforts to connect meaningfully with others.

One couple shared how understanding God's attributes transformed their marriage after years of conflict. "We were both raised with an image of God as primarily judgmental," the wife explained. "We brought that same critical spirit into our marriage, constantly focusing on each other's shortcomings."

As they began to grasp God's full character—His holiness balanced with mercy, His sovereignty exercised through love, His omniscience paired with grace—they started to relate differently to each other.

"We still hold each other accountable," the husband said, "but now it's from a foundation of acceptance rather than criticism. We've learned to balance truth with grace because that's how God relates to us."

8. Reclaim Cultural Engagement

Finally, understanding God's attributes transforms how we engage with culture—including politics, entertainment, social issues, and technological developments. Many Christians either withdraw from culture entirely (fearing contamination) or assimilate completely (losing distinctive witness). Neither approach reflects the fullness of God's character.

Consider how divine attributes might reshape cultural engagement:

- **Holy God**: Maintain distinctive values and practices without isolating from the broader culture. Recognize that being set apart doesn't mean being separated.

- **Unchanging God**: Hold to unchanging principles while adapting methods and approaches to changing contexts. Distinguish between timeless truth and time-bound applications.

- **Sovereign God**: Engage with confidence that God is working His purposes even through secular institutions and developments. Avoid both naive optimism and cynical pessimism about cultural trends.

- **Personal God**: Address issues and policies without dehumanizing those who hold different views. Remember that God engages personally with people across the political and cultural spectrum.

- **All-Knowing God**: Approach cultural conversations with humility, recognizing that no human perspective captures the full picture. Listen to diverse voices, especially those unlike your own.

- **Everywhere God**: Acknowledge God's presence in all cultural spheres—arts, entertainment, business, politics, sports—not just explicitly religious contexts. Look for divine fingerprints in unexpected places.

- **All-Powerful God**: Believe that God can work through minority voices and seemingly lost causes. Engage faithfully even when change seems impossible, trusting God's power rather than human strategies.

Understanding God's attributes helps us avoid both withdrawing from culture entirely and assimilating completely. I've seen this balanced approach lived out by a business leader in our community who serves on several civic boards. Rather than either imposing his faith aggressively or hiding it completely, he engages from a foundation of God's attributes.

"I don't compartmentalize my faith, but I also don't weaponize it," he told me. "I try to bring a perspective shaped by who God is— His holiness, wisdom, love, and power—to every conversation. Sometimes that means standing firm on certain issues. Other times it means finding unexpected common ground with people who don't share my beliefs."

His approach hasn't made him popular with everyone, but it has earned him respect across the political and religious spectrum. More importantly, it has allowed him to advance the common good while maintaining a distinctive witness to who God is.

> Understanding God's attributes helps us avoid both withdrawing from culture entirely and assimilating completely.

Integrated Response

These eight areas of application—daily awareness, identity alignment, decision-making, prayer patterns, suffering perspective, spiritual disciplines, relationship patterns, and cultural engagement—aren't isolated compartments. They're integrated aspects of a holistic response to who God is.

As you implement these practices, you'll likely notice a cascade effect. Greater awareness of God's attributes naturally reshapes your identity. A more secure identity influences decision-making. Better decisions affect relationships. Healthier relationships impact cultural engagement. Each area reinforces and amplifies the others.

The goal isn't perfect implementation but faithful response—not trying to earn God's approval through spiritual performance but aligning yourself increasingly with divine reality.

Remember my teenage preaching experience? The turning point came when I shifted from trying to impress to simply responding to what I'd experienced of God. That same principle applies to every aspect of faith. We aren't trying to manufacture spiritual maturity through our own efforts. We're responding to the God who has already revealed Himself to us.

As Peter reminds us, "His divine power has given us everything we need for a godly life through our knowledge of him who called us by his own glory and goodness. Through these he has given us his very great and precious promises, so that through them you may participate in the divine nature" (2 Peter 1:3–4 NIV).

God has already provided everything we need through what He's revealed about Himself. Our role is to respond in faithful alignment with that revelation. As we do, we find ourselves gradually "participating in the divine nature"—reflecting more and more of God's character in our daily lives.

This isn't instantaneous transformation but incremental conformation—becoming, step by step, more like the God we worship. The attributes we've explored aren't just theological concepts; they're invitations to participate in the very life of God.

Finding Your Next Step

As we conclude this chapter on practical application, you might be feeling overwhelmed by all the possible ways to respond to God's attributes. Where do you start? How do you move from information to implementation without getting lost in a sea of good intentions?

Let me suggest *a simple three-step process:*

1. Identify Your Current Challenge

What aspect of life is currently most challenging or confusing for you? It might be a relationship difficulty, a major decision, a persistent temptation, a painful circumstance, or a spiritual dry spell.

This current challenge is often the place God wants to meet you most immediately—not because He's limited to addressing one issue at a time, but because your awareness of need creates receptivity to His work.

2. Connect This Challenge to a Divine Attribute

Which attribute of God speaks most directly to your current challenge? For example:

- If you're facing constant change and instability, God's immutability might be most relevant.

- If you're struggling with feeling worthless or insignificant, God's personal knowing of you might be most needed.

- If you're facing an impossible situation, God's omnipotence might be most applicable.

- If you're wrestling with apparently unanswered prayer, God's sovereignty might be most important to grasp.

Don't overthink this connection. Often your initial instinct about which attribute seems most relevant is correct—it's the Holy Spirit guiding your attention to what you need most in this season.

3. Implement One Specific Response

Rather than trying to apply everything at once, choose one specific practice that connects your current challenge to the relevant divine attribute.

Make this practice concrete and measurable. Instead of "I'll trust God's sovereignty more," try "Each morning this week, I'll spend five minutes declaring specific truths about God's sovereignty over my current situation."

Keep the practice simple enough to be sustainable but specific enough to be meaningful. The goal isn't perfection but progress—not dramatic transformation but deliberate response.

A man in our church followed this process while facing a devastating job loss. His current challenge was obvious—unemployment, financial stress, and damaged self-worth. The divine attribute that seemed most relevant was God's immutability—that his value didn't change even when his employment status did.

His specific response was starting each day by writing down three truths about God's unchanging nature and three truths about his unchanging identity in Christ. This simple practice didn't instantly resolve his employment situation, but it provided an anchor for his soul during the transition.

"That daily declaration kept me from spiraling into despair," he told me. "It reminded me that while everything around me was changing, God wasn't changing, and my value to Him wasn't changing either."

Within six months, he found new employment—in a field that actually matched his gifts and calling better. Looking back, he recognized that God had used the painful transition to redirect his career path. But more importantly, he had developed a habit of grounding his identity in God's unchanging character rather than changing circumstances—a practice that would serve him in every future season.

Living from Encounter, Not Just Education

As we close this chapter on practical application, I want to return to where we began—with my teenage preaching experience and the lesson my youth pastor taught me: "Not showing people how much you know about God, but responding to what you've experienced of God."

The goal of understanding God's attributes isn't merely academic knowledge but personal encounter. We want to know about God so that we might know God—not just comprehend His qualities but experience His presence.

The Israelites at Mount Sinai had considerable theological knowledge about God. They had witnessed His plagues in Egypt, His parting of the Red Sea, His provision of manna in the wilderness. They had heard His voice thunder the Ten Commandments. Yet when Moses was delayed on the mountain, they quickly reverted to idol worship.

Why? Because they had information without transformation, education without encounter. They knew facts about God but hadn't been changed by relationship with God.

In contrast, Isaiah's encounter with God's holiness in the Temple (Isaiah 6) led to profound transformation. He didn't just learn about God's holiness; he experienced it. And that experience changed everything—his self-perception, his willingness to serve, his message to others.

As you apply what you've learned about God's attributes, pursue both accurate information and authentic encounter. Study diligently, but also create space for divine revelation. Learn theological concepts, but also listen for personal communication. Understand attributes intellectually, but also experience them relationally.

This balanced approach—valuing both the written Word and the living Spirit, both careful study and contemplative listening—provides the richest soil for spiritual growth. It prevents dry intellectualism on one hand and untethered emotionalism on the other.

It's what Paul prayed for the Ephesians: "I keep asking that the God of our Lord Jesus Christ, the glorious Father, may give you the Spirit of wisdom and revelation, so that you may know him better" (Ephesians 1:17 NIV). Notice the combination—wisdom (understanding) and revelation (encounter), all directed toward knowing God better.

This is my prayer for you as well—that your understanding of God's attributes would lead not just to better theology but to deeper relationship. That you would respond not just to what you've learned about God but to whom you've encountered in God.

For in the end, the most profound practical application of God's attributes is simply this: to know Him and to make Him known. To be transformed by His character and to reflect that character to a watching world.

May your response to who God is bring Him glory and you joy, today and in all the days to come.

Personal Reflection and Small Group Guide

Chapter Summary

This chapter translates theological understanding of God's attributes into practical application. Moving from knowing about God to living in response to Him, we explored eight areas of application: developing daily awareness practices, aligning identity with divine truth, transforming decision-making processes, reshaping prayer patterns, reframing suffering and challenges, revitalizing spiritual disciplines, renovating relationship patterns, and reclaiming cultural engagement. Rather than implementing everything at once, we're encouraged to identify our current challenge, connect it to a relevant divine attribute, and implement one specific response. The goal isn't perfect implementation but faithful response—not trying to earn God's approval through spiritual performance but aligning ourselves increasingly with divine reality, pursuing both accurate information and authentic encounter with God.

Key Scripture

"His divine power has given us everything we need for a godly life through our knowledge of him who called us by his own glory and goodness." (2 Peter 1:3 NIV)

Key Thought

"Theology isn't just for knowing; it's for living."

Personal Reflection

1. Of the seven divine attributes explored in this book (holiness, immutability, sovereignty, personal sovereignty, omniscience, omnipresence, omnipotence), which one has most significantly changed your understanding of God? How has this improved understanding affected your relationship with Him?

2. Look at the eight areas of practical application. In which area do you most need to align your life with what you now understand about God's attributes? What specific change would make the biggest difference?

3. Following the three-step process outlined in the chapter, identify your current biggest challenge. Which divine attribute speaks most directly to this challenge? What is one specific, measurable response you could implement this week?

4. The chapter discusses how our view of God shapes our approach to relationships. How has your understanding of God influenced how you relate to others? Is there a specific relationship pattern that needs renovation based on a more complete view of God's attributes?

5. Consider your prayer life. Which aspect of prayer discussed in this chapter (focusing on different divine attributes) represents the biggest gap in your current practice? How might incorporating this aspect enrich your communication with God?

6. Reflect on a recent difficult circumstance. How did you interpret it at the time? How might reframing it through the lens of God's attributes change your perspective and response?

7. The chapter emphasizes moving from information to encounter. When have you experienced God most personally, beyond intellectual understanding? What created the conditions for that encounter, and how might you cultivate similar opportunities?

Small Group Discussion

1. Jeff writes that "living in response rather than reaction" is key to applying our knowledge of God's attributes. Discuss the difference between reaction and response. Share examples of how you've seen this distinction play out in your own life.

2. Review the section on daily awareness practices together. Which practices seem most practical and meaningful for members of your group? How might you encourage and support each other in maintaining these practices?

3. Discuss how understanding God's attributes might reshape your group's approach to challenges and suffering. Share experiences of how viewing difficulties through the lens of God's character has transformed your perspective.

4. The chapter suggests that spiritual disciplines become richer when connected to specific attributes of God. Choose one discipline (Bible study, prayer, worship, or something else.) and discuss how understanding different facets of God's nature might revitalize this practice.

5. Consider the section on cultural engagement. How might your small group collectively reflect God's attributes in your community? What specific initiative or approach might allow you to maintain distinctive witness without either withdrawing from or assimilating to culture?

6. Pastor Jeff emphasizes the balance between accurate information and authentic encounter with God. How does your group currently encourage both? What adjustments might help create a better balance?

7. Share one specific application from this chapter that you plan to implement this week. How can group members pray for and support each other in these applications?

For Group Leaders

Preparation:

This chapter covers a wide range of practical applications. Before leading the discussion, identify which areas seem most relevant to your specific group based on their current season and challenges. Be prepared to guide the conversation toward concrete application rather than remaining in theoretical discussion.

Setting the Tone:

Begin by acknowledging that different personality types and spiritual temperaments will naturally gravitate toward different applications. Some may connect more easily with intellectual understanding, others with emotional experience, others with practical service. Affirm that these differences are by divine design, while encouraging everyone to grow in areas that don't come as naturally.

Facilitation Tips:

- For question #1 about which attribute has most changed their understanding, consider creating a visual representation—perhaps a poster with the seven attributes listed where people can place a mark beside the one that has most impacted them. This creates a visible picture of the group's collective experience.

- When discussing question #3 about current challenges, be sensitive that some members may not be comfortable sharing deeply personal struggles in the group setting. Offer the option of discussing in pairs or writing responses privately.

- For question #5 about prayer, consider implementing an attribute-focused prayer time during your meeting. Assign different attributes to different members and have each person lead a brief prayer focusing on that aspect of God's character.

- If discussing question #6 about suffering triggers painful emotions for some members, be prepared to provide appropriate pastoral care or referrals for additional support.

Application Focus:

End your time by having each person complete this sentence: "Based on what I've learned about God's attributes, this week I will..." Encourage specific, measurable commitments rather than vague intentions. Create accountability pairs within the group to follow up on these commitments before your next meeting. This transforms learning into living, knowledge into practice.

Conclusion
THE JOURNEY CONTINUES

ONE OF MY favorite places to visit in Jerusalem is the area near Caiaphas' house, where the Upper Room is believed to be. Right outside that area there's a large statue of King David playing the harp. It was a gift to Israel from the Russian Christian Orthodox Fund. It is a representation of King David as, "the sweetest psalmist of Israel."

King David is also described by others as being a man "after God's own heart." A man who, despite his failures and flaws, pursued intimate knowledge of God with rare passion. A man whose psalms still guide our worship and prayers thousands of years later.

When I stand near that statue, I always think about my own journey of life and faith. I don't mean to compare sin or compare worship. I just know that I've had many dark hours in my soul where I can identify God marking me through deep victories, defeats, mountain-top experiences and valley wanderings, big successes, and personal failures.

David's life wasn't a straight line of ever-increasing spiritual maturity. It was a winding path marked by moments of profound insight and instances of devastating blindness. Yet through it all, he kept returning to the fundamental question: Who is this God I serve?

In many ways, that's the question we've been exploring throughout this book. Who is God, really? Not just the God of our cultural assumptions or religious traditions, but the God who has revealed Himself through Scripture, creation, and most perfectly through Jesus Christ.

We've examined *seven essential attributes* that help us answer this question:

1. His **holiness** — His utter uniqueness and set-apartness

2. His **immutability** — His unchanging nature and character

3. His **sovereignty** — His supreme rule over all creation

4. His **personal sovereignty** — His engagement with human freedom

5. His **omniscience** — His complete and perfect knowledge

6. His **omnipresence** — His existence everywhere at the same time

7. His **omnipotence** — His unlimited power exercised with perfect control

Each attribute reveals something very important about who God is. Together, they provide a foundation for knowing and relating to the living God who created us, redeems us, and invites us into relationship with Him.

But as we conclude this exploration, I want to emphasize *three important truths about the journey of knowing God.*

1. The Journey Is Ongoing

First, our understanding of God is always growing, always deepening. No matter how much we've learned or experienced, there's always more to discover.

The apostle Paul, after years of remarkable ministry and profound revelation, still prayed "that I may know Him" (Philippians 3:10 NKJV). He recognized that knowing God isn't a destination we arrive at but a journey we pursue throughout our lives.

Scripture uses the metaphor of walking with God—an image of continuous movement and ongoing relationship. Enoch walked with God. Noah walked with God. Abraham walked before God. This language suggests progression, development, and deepening intimacy over time.

Even in Heaven, our knowledge of God will continue to expand. As finite beings, we'll never exhaust the infinite depths of who God is. For all eternity, we'll be discovering new facets of His character, new dimensions of His love, new expressions of His wisdom.

This ongoing nature of the journey should inspire both humility and anticipation. Humility because we recognize how much we still don't understand. Anticipation because there's always more to discover, more to experience, more to enjoy of God.

Whatever insights you've gained through reading this book, remember they're not the endpoint but simply markers along the path. The God who has revealed Himself to you thus far has infinitely more to show you in the days and years ahead.

2. The Journey Is Personal

Second, knowing God is inherently personal. While we can learn much about God through books, sermons, and theological study, true knowledge of God always includes direct, personal encounter.

The distinction is significant. You can know about a historical figure like Abraham Lincoln by reading biographies. But you cannot know Lincoln personally because you've never met him. With God, however, both dimensions of knowledge are possible and necessary—learning about Him and experiencing Him directly.

Jesus highlighted this distinction when He told the religious scholars of His day, "You study the Scriptures diligently because you think that in them you have eternal life. These are the very Scriptures that testify about me, yet you refuse to come to me to have life" (John 5:39–40 NIV). They had extensive knowledge about God but lacked personal relationship with God.

Throughout Scripture, we see how God reveals Himself uniquely to different individuals. He spoke to Moses from a burning bush. He revealed Himself to Elijah in a gentle whisper. He confronted Saul on the Damascus road. He appeared to John in apocalyptic vision.

While God's essential character never changes, how He manifests Himself to us often varies based on our unique personality, circumstances, and needs. The God who knows you completely also knows precisely how to make Himself known to you in ways you can perceive and respond to.

This personal dimension of knowing God means your journey won't look exactly like anyone else's. You may connect with certain attributes of God more readily than others. You may experience His presence through different means than your spouse, friend, or pastor does. You may hear His voice in ways unique to your relationship with Him.

These differences aren't signs that someone is doing it "right" and someone else "wrong." They're evidence that the infinite God relates to each of His finite creatures in ways tailored to their unique design.

> The infinite God relates to each of His finite creatures in ways tailored to their unique design.

3. The Journey Is Communal

Third, while knowing God is personal, it's not meant to be private. We discover and experience God most fully in community with other believers.

Scripture consistently presents spiritual growth as a communal process. Paul writes to the Ephesians that we are to "grow up in every way into him who is the head, into Christ, from whom the whole body, joined and held together by every joint with which it is equipped, when each part is working properly, makes the body grow so that it builds itself up in love" (Ephesians 4:15–16 ESV).

Note the interdependence here. Every part contributes to the growth of the whole body. No single member possesses complete understanding or experience of God. We need each other's perspectives, insights, gifts, and stories to see the full picture.

This is why isolating yourself from other believers is so dangerous. When you disconnect from the body, you cut yourself off from essential sources of divine revelation. God speaks not just directly to your heart but through the words, wisdom, and witness of others who know Him.

I've witnessed this reality countless times in our church community. Someone will share how they've experienced God's faithfulness through terrible loss, and suddenly others see dimensions of God's character they've never noticed before. A young believer will ask a question that causes longtime Christians to rethink assumptions they've held for decades. A child will express simple trust that shames sophisticated adults who've overcomplicated their faith.

As you continue your journey of knowing God, don't travel alone. Embed yourself in a community of fellow travelers who can help you see aspects of God's character you might miss on your own. Share your own discoveries and experiences to help others grow. Together, we paint a more complete portrait of the God who is too magnificent for any single perspective to fully capture.

From Knowledge to Transformation

The ultimate purpose of knowing God isn't just information accumulation but personal transformation. As Paul writes, "And we all, with unveiled face, beholding the glory of the Lord, are being transformed into the same image from one degree of glory to another" (2 Corinthians 3:18 ESV).

The more clearly we see who God is, the more fully we become who we're meant to be. Knowledge of God leads to conformity to Christ. Understanding divine attributes results in developing godly character. Theology, properly grasped, always leads to doxology (worship) and transformation.

This transformative power of knowing God explains why it's so essential to have an accurate, balanced understanding of His attributes. When we emphasize certain aspects of God's character while neglecting others, our spiritual development becomes similarly imbalanced.

If we focus exclusively on God's holiness without His mercy, we tend to become rigid and judgmental. If we emphasize His love without His justice, we drift toward permissiveness and moral compromise. If we stress His sovereignty without His goodness, we grow fatalistic and passive.

But when we embrace the full revelation of who God is—seeing all His attributes in their perfect harmony—we're transformed in ways that reflect this divine wholeness. We become more integrated, more balanced, more fully human in the truest sense of the word.

This transformation isn't instantaneous or automatic. It happens "from one degree of glory to another"—gradually, incrementally, often in ways we don't immediately recognize. But over time, as we continue to behold who God is, we can't help but become more like Him.

I saw this reality demonstrated in the life of two elderly saints in our congregation. Roger and Judy have known and walked with God for over seventy years. Their knowledge of Scripture is rich, their prayer life is steady, their wisdom has been tested by decades of experience of wins, joy, failure, loss, and pain.

What strikes me most about Roger and Judy isn't just what they know about God but how that knowledge had reshaped their perseverance and worship. Their understanding of God's character has produced remarkably vibrant faith and worship. When the sanctuary is packed, wall to wall and the full band and worship team are at full throttle, you can hear Roger and Judy singing over the whole crowd. If you catch a glimpse of them, their feeble arms and glowing faces are pointed straight to Jesus. Their grasp of His immutability has developed rock-solid stability amid life's changes. Their recognition of His sovereignty has fostered peaceful trust during painful losses. Their experience of His presence has created contagious joy that defies their physical limitations.

Roger and Judy haven't just accumulated information about God over the past seventy years. They have been increasingly transformed into His likeness. The attributes of God they have studied and experienced have gradually become attributes they reflect.

That's the invitation extended to each of us—not just to know about God but to be known by God, not just to understand divine attributes but to reflect them, not just to study God's character but to be changed by it.

> When we embrace the full revelation of who God is we're transformed in ways that reflect this divine wholeness.

Your Next Step

As we close this book, you might be wondering: *What now? Where do I go from here in this journey of knowing God more deeply?*

First, recognize that whatever understanding you've gained thus far is a gift from God, not something you've achieved through your own intellectual efforts. As Jesus told Peter when he recognized Jesus as the Messiah, "Blessed are you... for this was not revealed to you by flesh and blood, but by my Father in heaven" (Matthew 16:17 NIV). True knowledge of God always comes through revelation, not just education.

Second, respond to what you've already understood. Jesus taught that additional light comes to those who act on the light they've already received. "Whoever has will be given more, and they will have an abundance" (Matthew 25:29 NIV). Don't wait until you understand everything before you start applying what you already know.

Third, remain humble and teachable. The moment we think we've fully grasped who God is, we've diminished Him to something less than God. As Augustine famously said, "If you understand it, it is not God." Maintain the paradoxical position of confidently affirming what God has revealed while humbly acknowledging the limitations of your understanding.

Fourth, keep pursuing. The God who has revealed Himself to you wants to be known even more fully. He isn't hiding from you or playing hard to get. He's continuously inviting you deeper, revealing more of Himself as you're ready to receive it. As Jeremiah proclaimed, "You will seek me and find me when you seek me with all your heart" (Jeremiah 29:13 NIV).

My prayer for you as you close this book and continue your journey is the same one Paul prayed for the Ephesians: "That the God of our Lord Jesus Christ, the glorious Father, may give you the Spirit of wisdom and revelation, so that you may know him better" (Ephesians 1:17 NIV).

Not just know about Him. Know Him. Not just study His attributes. Experience His presence. Not just understand His character. Reflect His image.

For in the end, this is what we were created for—to know God and to make Him known, to be known by God and to be transformed by that knowing, to journey ever deeper into the infinite depths of who He is and to invite others to join in that glorious discovery.

The journey continues. And the God who has revealed Himself thus far has so much more to show you in the days ahead.

"Now to him who is able to do immeasurably more than all we ask or imagine, according to his power that is at work within us, to him be glory in the church and in Christ Jesus throughout all generations, for ever and ever! Amen" (Ephesians 3:20–21 NIV).

He is greater than you think.

Best Ahead.

Appendix 1

PRAYING THROUGH GOD'S ATTRIBUTES

AS WE CONCLUDE our exploration of God's attributes, we now turn from understanding to application, from theology to devotion. Knowledge about God that doesn't lead to communion with God remains merely academic. These prayers are designed to help you internalize the divine attributes we've studied and transform them from concepts in your mind to convictions in your heart.

Each prayer focuses on a specific attribute of God, helping you engage with that aspect of His character in a personal way. They follow a simple pattern: acknowledgment of who God is, thanksgiving for how that attribute impacts your life, petition for how it might transform you, and dedication to live in light of this truth.

These prayers aren't meant to be recited mechanically but prayed thoughtfully. Feel free to adapt them, personalize them, or use them as springboards for your own conversations with God. The accompanying Scripture references provide biblical foundations for each attribute.

May these prayers deepen your relationship with the God who is not just the subject of our study but the object of our worship—the One who is holy, unchanging, sovereign, all-knowing, ever-present, and all-powerful. As you pray through these attributes, may you not only know more about God but know Him more intimately.

Attribute-Focused Prayers

Prayer Focusing on God's Holiness

Holy Father, You stand apart from all creation—perfect in purity, complete in righteousness, transcendent above my limited understanding. I confess that I've often tried to make You more manageable, more predictable, more like myself. Forgive this subtle idolatry. Today I acknowledge Your absolute uniqueness. Set me apart for Your purposes, not my own agenda. Align my timing with Yours, my methods with Yours, my goals with Yours. Burn away whatever in me cannot stand in Your presence. Make my heart holy space where You can dwell. Let Your holiness flow through me, not to condemn the world but to transform it, one surrendered life at a time—beginning with mine. In the name of Jesus, who revealed perfect holiness in human form, Amen.

"But just as he who called you is holy, so be holy in all you do; for it is written: 'Be holy, because I am holy.'" (1 Peter 1:15-16 NIV)

Prayer Focusing on God's Immutability

Unchanging God, in a world where everything shifts and nothing seems secure, You remain the Rock that never moves. Your character doesn't fluctuate, Your promises don't fail, Your purposes don't waver. When my emotions rise and fall, when circumstances change without warning, when people prove unreliable—You are steadfast. I anchor my identity not in changeable factors but in Your unchanging love for me. I build my decisions not on shifting circumstances but on Your eternal principles. I find my security not in temporary stability but in Your permanent faithfulness. Thank You that I can trust who You were yesterday, who You are today, and who You'll be forever. In the name of Jesus Christ, the same yesterday, today, and forever, Amen.

"Jesus Christ is the same yesterday and today and forever." (Hebrews 13:8 NIV)

Prayer Focusing on God's Sovereignty

Sovereign Lord, You rule over all creation with perfect wisdom and complete authority. Nothing surprises You, nothing thwarts Your plans, nothing falls outside Your governance. When my world seems chaotic, remind me that You're still on the throne. When my circumstances appear hopeless, show me that You're still in control. When evil seems to triumph, assure me that You're still working all things for good. I surrender my need to understand everything, to control everything, to fix everything. Instead, I place my trust in Your sovereign wisdom and perfect timing. Give me the courage to follow where You lead, even when the path isn't what I would have chosen. In the name of Jesus, who submitted perfectly to Your sovereign will, Amen.

"The LORD has established his throne in heaven, and his kingdom rules over all." (Psalm 103:19 NIV)

Prayer Focusing on God's Personal Sovereignty

Gracious God, You are both sovereign over all creation and intimately engaged with every human heart. Thank You for respecting the freedom You've given me while still accomplishing Your purposes. Forgive me for the times I've demanded You take control in ways that align with my preferences rather than Your wisdom. Whether I struggle with safety fears, panic reactions, intellectual doubts, or stubborn resistance, meet me exactly where I am. Help me to trust that when You don't remove obstacles, You're providing strength to overcome them. When You don't change circumstances, You're changing me through them. Teach me to recognize Your voice calling my name, inviting me into deeper relationship with You. In Jesus' name, who perfectly modeled submission to Your will, Amen.

"Come to me, all you who are weary and burdened, and I will give you rest. Take my yoke upon you and learn from me, for I am gentle and humble in heart, and you will find rest for your souls." (Matthew 11:28-29 NIV)

Prayer Focusing on God's Omniscience

All-knowing Father, You perceive every thought before I think it, every word before I speak it, every action before I take it. Nothing about me surprises You—my failures, my fears, my doubts, my desires. You know me better than I know myself, yet You love me completely. I don't need to hide or pretend with You. I don't need to explain or defend myself. I can simply *be*, fully known and fully loved. Thank You for creating me as a unique masterpiece with a specific purpose. Thank You for seeing not just who I am now but who I'm becoming through Your grace. Help me find freedom in being known by You rather than fear. Help me extend to others the same grace You've shown to me. In the name of Jesus, who knows my heart perfectly, Amen.

"O LORD, you have searched me and you know me. You know when I sit and when I rise; you perceive my thoughts from afar... Before a word is on my tongue you, LORD, know it completely." (Psalm 139:1-2, 4 NIV)

Prayer Focusing on God's Omnipresence

Ever-present God, there is nowhere I can go where You are not already there. No circumstance can separate me from Your presence, no darkness can hide me from Your sight, no crisis can place me beyond Your reach. You inhabit both the heights of heaven and the depths of my daily routines. Thank You for Your universal presence that sustains all creation. Thank You for Your indwelling presence through Your Holy Spirit. Thank You for those special moments when You make Your presence known in tangible ways. Help me develop greater awareness of Your constant companionship. Transform me into a carrier of Your presence wherever I go—in my home, my workplace, my community. May others encounter something of You through my words, actions, and attitudes. In Jesus' name, whose life perfectly revealed Your presence, Amen.

"Where can I go from your Spirit? Where can I flee from your presence? If I go up to the heavens, you are there; if I make my bed in the depths, you are there." (Psalm 139:7-8 NIV)

Prayer Focusing on God's Omnipotence

Almighty God, all power belongs to You. Nothing is too difficult for You, no purpose of Yours can be thwarted, no promise of Yours will go unfulfilled. Yet Your power isn't expressed through brute force or cosmic bullying, but through perfect strength under perfect control. Like the Lion of Judah, You display authority and majesty. Like the Lamb who was slain, You demonstrate sacrifice and mercy. I marvel at both dimensions of Your power—creating galaxies and sustaining atoms, commanding oceans, and counting hairs, raising the dead, and responding to whispered prayers. When I face impossible situations, remind me that Your power is made perfect in my weakness. When I rely on my own strength, humble me to depend on Yours instead. Through Jesus Christ, who displayed both the power of the Lion and the sacrifice of the Lamb, Amen.

"I know that you can do all things; no purpose of yours can be thwarted." *(Job 42:2 NIV)*

Appendix 2
FOR ADDITIONAL STUDY
God's Attributes:
A Bibliography

Reader's Note: The following bibliography is offered as a reference resource for studying God's attributes from various Christian perspectives. Inclusion of a work does not constitute an endorsement of all theological positions held by its author. Readers are encouraged to engage thoughtfully with these texts, embracing helpful insights while exercising discernment regarding areas that may diverge from their own theological convictions. The beauty of Christian scholarship lies in the opportunity to learn from diverse voices while remaining grounded in Scripture and guided by the Holy Spirit.

———————

Blackaby, Henry and Richard. *Experiencing God: Knowing and Doing the Will of God.* A widely embraced work focusing on how God reveals Himself through relationship and invites believers to join Him in His work.

Carson, D.A. *The God Who Is There: Finding Your Place in God's Story.* Traces God's character through biblical theology, emphasizing God's sovereignty while remaining accessible to various Christian traditions.

Chan, Francis. ***Forgotten God: Reversing Our Tragic Neglect of the Holy Spirit.*** Examines the Holy Spirit with balanced perspectives acceptable to a wide range of conservative Christians.

Foster, Richard J. ***Prayer: Finding the Heart's True Home.*** Explores different dimensions of prayer that connect with God's attributes.

Hayford, Jack. ***The Knowledge of the Holy Spirit.*** Explores God's attributes with particular emphasis on the Holy Spirit's presence and power.

Johnson, Bill. ***Face to Face with God.*** Focuses on experiencing God's presence, connecting His attributes to personal spiritual encounters.

Lawrence, Brother. ***The Practice of the Presence of God.*** A classic focusing on God's omnipresence in daily life.

Lewis, C.S. ***Mere Christianity.*** Though not exclusively about God's attributes, provides profound insights into God's nature from a broadly accepted perspective.

McGrath, Alister. ***Understanding the Trinity.*** Explores the triune nature of God in ways that are accessible.

McKnight, Scot. ***The King Jesus Gospel.*** Presents God's character as revealed in the gospel story.

Nouwen, Henri. ***The Return of the Prodigal Son.*** A meditation on God's unconditional love and mercy through the lens of Rembrandt's painting and Jesus' parable.

Packer, J.I. ***Knowing God.*** A widely embraced work on God's attributes that combines theological precision with devotional warmth.

Tozer, A.W. *Knowledge of the Holy.* A profound exploration of God's attributes that has become a spiritual classic, accessible yet deep.

Warren, Rick. *The Purpose Driven Life.* While not exclusively about God's attributes, it explores God's intentionality, wisdom, and relational nature in accessible terms.

Willard, Dallas. *Hearing God: Developing a Conversational Relationship with God.* Explores God's communicative nature from a perspective that bridges evangelical and contemplative traditions.

www.ingramcontent.com/pod-product-compliance
Lightning Source LLC
Chambersburg PA
CBHW060415130626
46555CB00005B/2076